Successful Freelancing

THE COMPLETE GUIDE
TO ESTABLISHING AND RUNNING
ANY KIND OF FREELANCE BUSINESS

Revised Edition

MARIAN FAUX

St. Martin's Press ✻ New York

SUCCESSFUL FREELANCING. Copyright © 1982, 1996 by Marian Faux. All rights reserved. Printed in the United States of America. No part of this book may be used or reproduced in any manner whatsoever without written permission except in the case of brief quotations embodied in critical articles or reviews. For information, address St. Martin's Press, 175 Fifth Avenue, New York, N.Y. 10010.

Design by Irving Perkins Associates, Inc.

ISBN 0-312-15215-9

First Edition: April 1997

D 10 9 8 7 6 5 4 3 2

P1

FOR MY PARENTS,
who encouraged me and taught me to think of freelancing
as the serious business that it is

Contents

Acknowledgments

Although I have freelanced for many years, I could not have written this book without the help of other freelancers, who shared their experiences and information with me in most generous ways. I am especially indebted to the following people, who also gave generously of their time: Sharon Kapnick, Bryan Johnson, Barbara Zimmerman, Nicol Knappen, and Deborah Drier.

Special thanks go to Shelley Martin, a partner at Weikart Tax Associates, who read the tax chapter for accuracy and also offered many excellent suggestions.

I shall always be grateful to my parents, both good business managers, who taught me the importance of a well-run business. Finally, thanks go to my husband, Bill Willig, who among his other talents keeps me up-to-date on technology.

FOREWORD

OVER THE LAST SEVERAL YEARS, THE RANKS of the freelancer have swelled massively in numbers and in diversity. The self-sufficient lifestyle of the independent entrepreneur is a way whose time has come. There are three reasons for the expansion of freelancing. First, larger companies, in an attempt to reduce overhead, have farmed out many operations formerly executed by in-house staff. Independent professionals in advertising, sales, writing, design, graphics services, and many other areas have benefited from this tilt toward outside expertise.

The second major reason for the upsurge in freelancing stems from the astonishing development of unusual services. My own specialty of organizer did not exist ten years ago; neither did the profession of the wardrobe analyst, the "surrogate wife," and many other one-person service enterprises. My guess is that these services will continue to expand, especially in professions that lift some household burdens from the harassed two-career family.

And third, the increasingly footloose and free tone of our society encourages people with distinctive skills to set off on their own. People can make their way across the country—or throughout the world for that matter—as independent computer programmers, word processors, tutors, translators, and dog groomers.

With this growth in numbers and diversity comes the recognition that freelancing is a serious business with potential for earning substantial income. In order to realize that potential, while enjoying the freedom that was probably the impetus to go independent in the first place, what does the freelancer need to know? The chief requirements are: how to identify prospective clients; how to market oneself; how to make proposals or presentations; how to clinch sales; how to negotiate fees; how to handle contractual arrangements and legal responsibilities; and how to run an office and find extra help when needed. And perhaps most important, one must be able to coolly assess the traits of temperament and personality that are necessary for a successful freelance life.

Until now, each freelancer has had to work out the answers for these questions by trial and error, reinventing the wheel, so to speak, because there was no body of knowledge or communal experience on which to draw. Marian Faux's *Successful Freelancing* fills that gap in two ways: by addressing the issues raised above, and many others, thoroughly and with clarity, and by forging out of the strands of experience of many individual practitioners the sense that the freelancer's option is indeed a viable career choice, and that the freelancer, though independent, is not alone. This book is a welcome addition to the library of anyone who is—or is thinking of becoming—a freelancer.

STEPHANIE WINSTON
Author of *Getting Organized: The Easy Way to Put Your Life in Order*

INTRODUCTION TO THE
SECOND EDITION

WHAT'S A FREELANCER? THE ANSWER TO THIS question has changed enormously since I wrote the first edition of this book. Then, a freelancer was someone who worked in the arts or in publishing or who was engaged in an offbeat occupation such as dog walker or house sitter. Independent souls, these freelancers tended to buy into a lifestyle as much as they sought a lifelong career. Many freelancers were not particularly businesslike, nor did they expect to earn big money.

But since then freelancing has turned into something entirely different. Today's freelancers are businesslike, even corporate, in their approach to their work. They still like their independence, and they don't mind staying small. Many even cherish the chance to run a home-based business. They expect to earn big money, they are eager to expand their businesses, and they are very profit-oriented.

Ten years ago, freelancing tended to be a young person's occupation. Now it draws people of all ages. Large numbers of baby boomers, disenchanted with corporate life, are starting over with freelance careers. Freelancing makes sense at several other stages of life as well. Women who want to keep a hand in the workplace while they rear children turn to freelancing and often end up freelancing for a lifetime. Retirees who are not quite ready to quit working often cap off successful careers with an even more successful freelance business.

Freelancing attracts more women than men. For every man who starts his own freelance operation, three women do. Minorities are also drawn to freelancing, perhaps for the same reasons women are. There are no glass ceilings in freelancing; the only limits are those you impose on yourself.

In addition to the changing demographics of American life, computers have revolutionized freelancing. Thanks to computers and other new technology, many new opportunities to freelance now exist. Computers have expanded the numbers of people working at home to 25 million and growing. Work that only a decade ago had to be done in an office is now done faster and better at home. Computers have created new pockets of need. All the new home-based businesses need services and support, which creates a need for still more freelance businesses.

Computers have streamlined and simplified the operation of freelance businesses, and they have taken much of the monotony out of such tasks as bookkeeping and sales. In doing this, they have made freelancing more attractive than ever to creative people. But freelancing is no longer the special province of the creative person. Today's freelancer is just as likely to be an art consultant, lawyer, physician, stockbroker, financial services manager, or computer technician as an editor or an artist.

In response to these changes, a great deal of new material has been added to this book. An entirely new chapter discusses freelancers' special relationship to technology. Another new chapter focuses on business plans, which are important to any profit-oriented career. Since freelancing is now a lifetime proposition for greater numbers of people than ever before, another new chapter focuses on establishing a benefits program. The material on legal structures also has been expanded, as has the material on marketing.

The number of self-employed persons is expected to continue to grow well into the twenty-first century. If companies continue to remain competitive by laying off workers, freelancing ironically may become one of the most stable means of employment as workers conclude that they can do as well if not far better working for themselves. The goal of this book is to help those who do choose a career in freelancing to run the most successful businesses they can.

Successful Freelancing

1

THE FREELANCER'S GAME

THE AGE OF THE SELF-EMPLOYED PERSON is upon us. After a century of decline, the number of self-employed has been steadily and significantly rising since the 1970s. With corporate layoffs more common than perhaps any time in the past, increasing numbers of people are turning to self-employment. Home-based businesses, for many decades a very small percentage of the self-employed, have also been enjoying a resurgence. Demographers believe that the number of freelancers will grow steadily throughout the next two or three decades.

The trend toward more freelancers is part of an emerging new pattern in employment. People who formerly worked at one profession their entire lives, rarely changed jobs, and retired at the ripe young age of sixty-five now change careers (often several times), frequently change jobs, and retire later and later. Given these social changes, it is inevitable that more people will turn to freelancing, either temporarily or permanently, in the next few decades.

Those who take early retirement often forge entirely new second careers. Women who feel they have commitments at home often freelance. Men and women who have gotten into the corporate rat race and suffered the consequences often find that they want out, and freelancing offers a way. And the more relaxed work ethic that emerged in the 1960s, which decreed that people had a right to expect satisfaction from their work, has been enough to catapult many people into their own freelance enterprises.

GETTING AT THE HEART OF FREELANCING

More than any other career choice, freelancing suffers from being ill-defined. Many people don't understand what sets a freelancer apart from other small businesses. And freelancers themselves often have trouble describing what it is they do.

One woman, a freelance photographer's representative for several years, half wails, "A lot of the time, I think people on the outside have no idea what on earth freelancers do. I'm sure my mother hasn't got a clue what I do." A freelance writer who spends hours doing research in various university libraries says, "Whenever I tell someone that I'm currently working in a library, he says, 'Oh, did you get a job?' "

By most definitions, a freelancer is someone who sells services—specifically his or her own—rather than a product. It is typically a one-person operation, although some freelance businesses grow enough so there is a need to hire others, especially support staff to help them better provide services. A freelance operation is often, but not always, a home-based business. The most common form of legal organization is an unincorporated sole proprietorship, but freelancers also form partnerships, and some choose to incorporate.

Some professions traditionally have supported many freelancers—publishing and theater are two of the better examples. Musicians, artists, and writers often freelance because there is no other way to run their professional lives. But many teachers freelance. So do librarians, fashion designers, photographers, models, public relations people, therapists, computer specialists, financial planners, professional shoppers, and many people who work in the media. Consulting is nothing but a fancy word for freelancing.

Apart from not selling products, several psychological differences separate small-business owners from freelancers. Small-business owners are often people who seek the American dream of owning and operating their own businesses, who believe in Horatio Alger and success and ambition. Freelancers, on the other hand, are more likely to be driven by the opposite impulse: dreams of freedom and independence. They do not want to create pint-sized domains similar to the ones where they have worked all their lives; they want to get away from the organized and highly structured world of business.

Barbara Zimmerman, who has carved out a comfortable niche for herself as a freelance copyright editor, subscribes to this idea: "I think there is a difference between people who freelance and people who run small businesses, even though running a small business is a high form of freelancing. It would be interesting to know why someone chooses one over another. I think freelancers want their freedom, and that governs a lot of what they do."

A freelance set designer talked about the issue of independence, saying, "I watched my father run a small business. He had employees, he worried about payroll, and he bought turkeys for people at holiday time. He was his own boss in one sense, yet his time was not his own. He had obligations. I hate the thought that I might someday have to hire a secretary or an assistant. I like my independence, my smallness. I may have responsibilities, but I have few obligations. I'd like to keep it that way."

Lots of freelancers are independent and sometimes antiauthoritarian souls. They may not have been outwardly rebellious when they worked for someone else, but most simply never felt comfortable in offices. Stephanie Winston, a freelance professional organizer, recalls those feelings: "The real reason I left my job was that I don't accept authority easily. I don't like other people telling me what to do. Some people who don't deal easily with authority get rebellious, but I didn't do that. I got withdrawn. A boss can be the most benevolent authority in the world, and I still don't like his authority. I realized that as soon as I took my first job out of college. I didn't know how I would get out, but I knew I would—so that's why I knew I would grab the chance to freelance."

Barbara Lee, a soft-spoken photographer's representative, shares similar feelings: "I fell into freelancing when I knew I couldn't stand working for anyone else again. The man I worked for fired me right after I returned from a vacation because he couldn't afford me. He said he could hire someone cheaper than me to do the paperwork. Then, the following spring, he called me and said, 'Well, are you ready to come to work again? Are you ready for another season?' I probably would not have taken the plunge if I had not been fired.

"I had been fired a couple of times. This was not the first time. I kept thinking, I'm a nice, conservative, upstate New York girl. Why is it that I'm getting fired? The reason was that I resented the bureaucracy. I resented the paperwork. I found it difficult to work with people stupider than myself. I'm not usually abrasive, at least not when I'm comfortable. But put me in a position where I'm up against the wall, and I do rebel. On Monday morning, when I have to appear someplace, I'm up against the wall. It was a ridiculous way to live."

BUILDING A SMALL BUSINESS

Finally, there is for most freelancers the issue of size. Unlike small businesses, which are often eager to grow into big ones, freelancers are usually small, proud of it, and determined to stay that way. Even rich, successful freelancers like to keep things simple. They are not eager to hire staff, get a bigger office, or franchise.

This fact, however, should not prevent a freelancer from running a businesslike operation. In truth, far more is expected of most freelancers than of other small-business owners. Because we like to stay small, we wear many different hats, not just when we are growing, but for as long as we operate our freelance enterprises. Successful freelancers understand that they have to be part accountant, part executive, part supply clerk, and even part therapist (to themselves!) to keep a freelance operation afloat. Because of this, it's important to ask yourself, before you start freelancing, whether this is really the job for you.

Pros and Cons of Freelancing

Freelancing has many advantages but the primary ones might be summarized as follows:

- If you run your freelance career like a business, you have better than a fifty-fifty chance of achieving financial success.
- When you work for yourself, there is, in theory, no limit to the amount of money you can earn. What you earn will depend on your time, talent, and commitment.
- You will have the freedom and independence to plan your own work and organize your own time.
- You will have an enormous sense of fulfillment, personally and professionally.
- You will enjoy freedom from control by others. There is no boss to tell you what to do and when to start, no company policy to establish your vacations or holidays.
- You will own your work. A newspaper reporter who went to work as press aide for a senator quickly realized that he was turning out a huge amount of written material and getting credit for none of it. "Since much of it was fiction anyway," he joked, "I decided I might as well write some fiction on my own. So I began my life as a freelance writer."
- You can work out of your home or close to home, which means you have fewer commuting costs—and far less stress than the average commuter.
- You can work in two or more fields at once.
- You will enjoy flexibility. You can, for example, work odd hours if that is your style, although most freelancers, like any business owner, find that they need to be available during normal business hours. But you can work a ten-hour day, a four-day week, or any other configuration that suits you and still lets you get your work done.
- Your family life will be enhanced. Freelancers work very hard,

but most are home-based, and this, along with the ability to control their own work hours, often means more time for family life.

- You will enjoy relative simplicity. Even though this book offers many suggestions for ways to organize and manage your freelance career, they are made with an eye toward preserving simplicity.

And there are some disadvantages, too:

- The hours are long, especially when you start. Although they taper off as you become more successful and charge more for your services, many freelancers report that they must undertake periods of heavy work. There is no one to share the work with.
- There is paperwork and record keeping in any kind of freelance business. When you start, you have to put together and maintain your own benefits package, something your boss formerly did for you. You should write a business plan. You have to maintain financial records for the IRS. And you probably have to maintain a set of records related to your clients.
- Freelancing can be lonely. Freelancers spend many hours, sometimes days, alone. Even freelancers such as artists' and advertisers' representatives, who spend many hours each week calling on people to obtain work, say the contact they have with people does not compare with the camaraderie of daily office work—and many report that this kind of social contact is more frustrating than none at all.
- It may at times be hard to regulate your cash flow—a particularly stressful problem. No one pays you every two weeks or once a month, and often freelancers are owed a lot of money at the very time they are struggling to figure out how to pay the rent.
- The responsibility is sizable; there is no one to pass the buck to. If something goes wrong, *you* fouled it up. That is more responsibility than some people want to cope with. In addition, you must take responsibility for all the benefits your former employer supplied.

THE ISSUE OF SECURITY

Many people feel that freelancers have less job security than those who enjoy the comforts of a full-time job. But this need not be the case—and in these days of corporate layoffs, it often is not the case. Barbara Zimmerman, a freelance researcher, recalls the moment she decided she would feel more secure working for herself: "The company I worked for was sold. They tossed a coin to see who would get fired. They fired an outstanding executive who was fifty-five and had four kids in college. I said to myself, This could happen to me. And I decided to freelance before it did."

Freelance life need not be insecure. Successful managers learn how to plan work so there is no slowdown. They figure out how to maintain an even cash flow. Freelancers also have all the financial tools that enable one to plan a secure retirement as well as the more immediate future.

REASONS TO FREELANCE

Apart from the advantages and disadvantages, there are many things that drive a person to give freelancing a try:

You dislike the restrictive atmosphere in an office.
Your present work is boring.
You are independent.
You lack job advancement opportunities in your field.
You are unemployed.
You want postretirement work.
You want to earn more money.
You won't be promoted anymore in your present job.
You welcome a chance to test your entrepreneurial abilities and
    creativity.
You want a chance to love your work.

ARE YOU THE TYPE?

To freelance, you need three things: skills, background, and the right personality. Before setting out to freelance, you should do some serious self-analysis to make sure you have the right combination of these traits to be successful.

Skills and Background: How to Get Them

Except in rare fields where you can apprentice as you freelance, you must acquire the necessary skills and background before you go to work for yourself. For most people, this means years rather than months of working for someone else. You need the benefit of the evaluation you receive from others more experienced than you and of a work setting where you can learn from your mistakes without paying a personal—often financial—price.

In addition to specific work skills and background, a certain amount of sales and managerial ability is needed. Many freelancers lack business experience; if you are one of these people, take a few courses in management and business before you strike out on your own.

The following brief quiz will help you evaluate whether you have the necessary skills and background to freelance:

_____   Have you worked in an area where you hope to freelance for at least five years and preferably longer?

_____   Have you acquired any new skills you need to freelance?

_____   Are you willing to work long hours? Weekends?

_____   Have you had any business training, or will you get some before you start freelancing?

_____   If you will eventually hire employees, have you ever worked as a manager?

Do You Have a Freelancer's Personality?

Certain personality traits are also helpful in order to freelance successfully. You need lots of self-confidence, plus an ability to withstand rejection. You need good negotiating skills. One freelance editor-writer points out that the ability to tolerate isolation is one of the more important traits a freelancer needs: "You not only have to be able to work alone, but you have to be able to discipline yourself when no one is looking over your shoulder. The rest of the world generally thinks you have much more freedom than you actually have. Friends will call you just to chat. They will expect you to be free in the afternoon when they are in from out of town or simply need to talk to someone about their career problems. You have to say no to most of these requests, just as you would if you worked for someone else."

Freelance librarian Bryan Johnson says, "You need an ability to organize your time, but at the same time, an ability to stay flexible. Also, the ability to take pressure is important. Freelancers can bite off more than they can handle. You can have four jobs due on Friday, and here it is Wednesday already." Barbara Lee points out another trait that most freelancers need: "I have an ability to say no. That helps in freelancing. One of my photographers wanted me to work out of his office. I said absolutely not. I knew he worked fourteen hours a day, and I couldn't. My end of the business did not require that. I figured he didn't need to see me on a slow or nonproductive day. Most important, though, I simply know how to say no."

Freelance editor Sharon Neely thinks an ability to tolerate money pressures is important, as do many freelancers. Neely reports: "I think the money is the biggest thing. There are times when money doesn't come in because you haven't done anything. Those times are rare, though, if you are diligent about pursuing work. But then, there are times when you have done a lot of work and people owe you thousands of dollars, but they aren't paying you. It can make for sleepless nights, and you'll get an ulcer if you don't learn to handle that kind of pressure."

Although only you can decide if you have the personality traits you need to succeed at freelancing, the following quiz may provide some things to think about:

1. _____ Do you like other people? Even if you work alone, you still have to sell yourself, and to do that, you must like others.

2. _____ Do you welcome responsibility? You had better, since you are the chief, the only chief, in your business.

3. _____ Are you a leader? Leadership may not sound like a trait required of someone who works alone, but it is imperative. It is what will make you a self-starter.

4. _____ Do you make decisions easily? You will have lots to make, so you had better be decisive.

5. _____ Are you a hard worker? This is a necessity, possibly for a long stretch of time.

6. _____ Are you highly organized? Again, this is a necessary ingredient for success.

7. _____ Are you a self-starter? Freelancers do not sleep late, take two-and-a-half-hour lunches, or go to the movies every afternoon at four o'clock. They force themselves to stay inside and work even when they want to be somewhere else.

8. _____ Are you disciplined? Can you set and keep regular hours? Will you miss your boss prodding you to make deadlines?

9. _____ Are you outgoing enough to sell yourself?

10. _____ Are you healthy? Stamina counts for a lot when you freelance since there is no paid sick leave.

11. _____ Are you resourceful? Will you know what to do when you hit a slump? For that matter, will you know what to do when more work than you can handle comes pouring in?

12._____ Can you live with insecurity?

13._____ Can you live without praise or much reassurance from superiors? Almost no one calls a freelancer to say that a job was well done.

14._____ Can you stand constant pressure to find work?

15._____ Are you willing to forgo promotions and raises as signs that you have done a good job?

If you answered yes to ten or more of these questions, you are ready to freelance, and the next step is to start planning your business. Before you take the leap, though, you need to write a business plan. That's where you find out whether your idea for a business is a good one and whether you have enough money to start a business. You should be able to answer yes to both these questions before giving up your present job.

2

GETTING STARTED: THE BUSINESS PLAN

MOST FREELANCERS WOULDN'T DREAM OF WRITING A business plan. They protest that their businesses are too small to warrant one or that they aren't likely to obtain a bank loan in any event. Since obtaining a bank loan is, at least in most people's minds, the primary reason to labor over a business plan, why bother? But these aren't the only or even the most important reasons to write one.

The real reason is to figure out what business you are in, or should be in. In our fantasy lives, we all get to start the business of our dreams, but in the real world, we sometimes have to settle for a business that actually enables us to earn a living. Or we do get to open the business of our dreams, but first we must fine-tune it so that it will be truly viable. A business plan helps you—indeed, forces you—first to consider whether you really can be in the business you want to be in. And if your business idea is viable, then a business plan helps you develop it as fully as possible, which in turn maximizes profits.

Consider Cynthia, a preschool teacher with impeccable credentials, who after five years of teaching in the public school system and seven of teaching in someone else's preschool decided it was time to strike out on her own. The mother of a two-year-old, Cynthia saw many advantages to starting a preschool in her home. She longed to operate a home-based business and believed she lived in the ideal place to do so. Cynthia owned a spacious farmhouse situated on five green, rolling acres ten miles outside a small midwestern town with a population of 50,000. Initially she even thought she would install the school in her house, but as she grew more enthusiastic about her idea, she expanded it to include a separate schoolhouse on her grounds.

Moving full force ahead, Cynthia took out a business loan from the teachers' union, which did not require her to have a business plan. She used the money to build and equip a charming schoolhouse, install an above-ground pool, and buy sturdy gym equipment.

Cynthia talked about her idea with friends, acquaintances, and family and always got an enthusiastic response. Two months before she was due to open, she advertised in the local newspaper and even enticed a local reporter to interview her in her fine new schoolhouse.

Four months later, Cynthia's schoolhouse sat empty, an expensive and painful reminder of a venture that had not taken off. When enrollment started, Cynthia had drawn the interest of ten parents, only seven of whom ultimately had enrolled their preschoolers in her school. A small class would suit her, she had decided, and besides, she believed enrollment would build as word circulated about what a lovely setting the school was in.

But one month after the school opened, when Cynthia had to make her first loan payment, she finally sat down to figure out how many students she needed to be able to repay her loan, let alone earn a living. To her shock, she discovered that she required at least twenty students. The school immediately closed its doors. Devastated and in debt, Cynthia began the painful postmortem on her business. What had gone wrong?

For one thing, she had never seriously analyzed her customers. Yes, friends and acquaintances had said they would love to have her teach their children, but when the chips were down, most harried parents were not willing to drive the twenty-mile daily round-trip to put their children in her school, especially when there was an older, more established one operated by her former employer and conveniently located in town.

Cynthia never surveyed the competition. She hadn't weighed how popular or established her former employer was, nor had she bothered to learn that still another preschool was opening its doors at the same time she started her school. This school, run by a relative newcomer to the area, was located in town.

Finally, she did not do the necessary math to learn whether she needed a loan, and more important, whether she would be able to pay it back. Had she done this, she would have discovered far earlier how many students she needed to pay back the loan. And when she learned that, she would also have realized that she would need to hire another person to help her operate the school, another major expense.

All these problems could have been avoided or resolved had Cynthia taken the time to write a business plan. With this in hand, Cynthia would have discovered that her idea, at least as she initially framed it, was simply not viable. However much she wanted to, she could not earn a living operating a preschool located at her house. Discouraging as it would have been to discover this, all would not have been lost and certainly she need not have plunged so deeply in debt.

Before investing a cent in the business or taking out a loan, Cynthia would have learned that she had two options: to give up the idea of the preschool and find another home-based business to operate, if that is what she wanted to do; or to move the preschool to a more desirable location. Cynthia was a popular teacher, and while she could not have taken all of her former employer's business, she could have drawn more business than the other new school had she been more accessible.

Instead, like many people who simply jump into a new business without much planning, Cynthia found herself on a sinking ship. Fifty thousand dollars in debt and stuck with a specialized building outfitted for a very specific purpose, she had no choice but to abandon her dream. When she belatedly explored other home-based businesses, she found she could not afford to operate one because she was too deeply in debt, and the expense of converting the schoolhouse would be too great.

The experience of writing a business plan always develops you as a manager. In fact, it is one way of testing your mettle before actually starting a business.

First and foremost, though, writing a business plan helps you figure out whether your business idea is feasible. If on closer examination, your idea does not seem as practical as you first thought it was, then a business plan may help you fine-tune the idea.

The act of writing a business plan may cause you to give up on one idea and investigate another. Painful as this may be, at least you will have tossed out the bad idea before taking out a bank loan or investing any of your hard-earned savings.

Once you have decided that your idea is indeed a solid one, the other important purpose of a business plan is to figure out how much money you will need to start the business. If you do not have enough money, you will see what size loan you need. If you realize you do not have the funding for the business, nor are you likely to obtain it from a lender, a business plan can show you how you may still be able to salvage your idea. But first let's see what goes into a business plan.

RESEARCHING THE BUSINESS PLAN

All business plans begin with research. Cynthia was smart to talk to family and friends about her idea, but she didn't take her research far enough. She might actually have created a written poll to survey such things as parents' work habits, their willingness to drive several miles to a school, even their loyalty to their present school.

Cynthia could also have checked out more formal sources of information such as the local Chamber of Commerce, the small-business center at a nearby university, the Small Business Administration, the business section of her local library.

From these sources, she would have learned a great deal that would have helped her in planning her business. From the Chamber of Commerce she would have obtained important demographics about her community that would have enabled her to assess whether the community could support one more preschool, let alone two. Advisers at the small-business center would have insisted that she work on her finances at a far earlier stage of planning, and she would have known how many students she needed to become profitable. She would have learned that with that number of students, she would need to hire someone to work for her, which in turn would mean that she had to earn still more money to pay an employee or take out a larger loan.

Had she been reading the business pages of her local newspaper, she would have learned earlier that she had more competition than she thought. In addition, the librarian might well have pointed her toward the census, a valuable planning tool to any prospective business owner. With it she would have learned exactly how many preschool children there were in her community, an important statistic that might have influenced her decision, as well as what their parents' incomes were and thus whether they could afford her services.

Finally, the information that she gained from her research would have led her to analyze her location in far more depth. And she would have concluded much sooner that she was unlikely to operate a successful preschool in her preferred location.

Many other resources are available to the prospective freelancer who is in the early investigative stages of testing an idea. Here are some sources of information for exploring your business idea:

- Attend the small-business fairs that are sponsored several times a year in most large cities.
- Check out small-business classes and/or seminars offered at local universities, as well as specialized help available at small-business centers that many universities operate.
- Talk to experts, including your competition. Obviously information gleaned from competitors should be taken with a grain of salt, since few will wholeheartedly welcome more competition, but this doesn't mean you should rule out competitors as a source of information. A friendly business lunch (you pay) often yields several important pieces of information.
- Chambers of Commerce. They are excellent sources of community demographics.

- The public library. Most libraries have on-line information and important demographics and statistics that are helpful to anyone who is investigating a new business. Best of all is a library with a business department. These exist in cities and universities.
- The census. Large libraries usually have the census. You may think of this as only information the federal government gathers on its citizenry every ten years, but in fact the Department of Commerce publishes a steady stream of information, based on the census, about U.S. businesses. You can also look up valuable information and demographics on your community, such as how many homeowners there are, age of population, number of children, etc.
- Bankers. Your banker is a good source of informal but very helpful information. He or she will know how your competitors are doing, whether any businesses like yours are also in the start-up stages, and most important, whether you are likely to get a loan.
- Accountants. In the planning stages of any business, it is helpful to talk with an accountant, preferably one with some knowledge of the kind of business you hope to start. This is where your other research becomes concrete, where you can apply the information you have gathered to the business you hope to start.

This period of gathering information is also an ideal time to brush up on business-operating skills. Many freelancers, for example, have specific skills that pertain to their career but lack the more general skills, such as selling or accounting, that are also necessary to run a small business. It helps to take classes and seminars designed to build up these skills as well.

WRITING THE BUSINESS PLAN

At some point during your investigations, you will have enough information to begin writing a business plan. If this step feels intimidating, as it does for most people, keep in mind that at least initially the business plan is your personal managerial tool. No one else will see it, so don't worry about whether you write well or whether you have all the information. It is important only that you get the information you have gathered down on paper so you can examine it and begin to draw some conclusions.

Start with something familiar or an area of the business toward which you feel a special affinity. Maybe you are dying to write a description of your customers because you have gathered so much interesting information about them. Or perhaps you have found out fascinating things about your competition. If so, this is the place to begin. Save the financial section for last since it is for most people the most daunting part of the business plan.

One question that often comes up is whether you can use a computer software program to do this. There are some programs designed for writing business plans, but none are geared to freelance operations. Nor will you need to write as complex and sophisticated a plan as someone who is starting, for example, a clothing manufacturing business. Therefore, most of the computer programs on writing business plans will not work for you. But your work certainly will be easier if you write on a computer and use a word-processing program. Using a spreadsheet will also be helpful when you start crunching numbers, because you can plug in different sets of numbers to see how each works.

THE COMPONENTS OF A BUSINESS PLAN

Business plans are composed of several parts. In fact, it may be helpful to think of a business plan as a series of minireports.

Not all of the minireports apply to every business. For example, if you are starting a business that is unique, you may not have any competitors and thus will have no need to write a competitors' profile. (Such businesses are extremely rare, though.) Similarly, if you are the president, manual laborer, cleaning person, and file clerk, it is pointless to draw up an organizational plan.

Don't make the mistake, though, of thinking you can skip the financial section of a business plan just because you are not planning to seek a bank loan. There are, as you will see in the next few pages, many important financial decisions to be made about a new business even when you are starting it with your own funds. It is still extremely important to do the financial calculations, perhaps even more important. With a bank loan, you are using someone else's money, but if you are relying on your own savings, as over 90 percent of all people who start freelance operations do, then it is your money that is at risk. This should be reason enough to prepare a solid financial section.

Here are the components, or minireports, that make up a typical business plan:

OVERVIEW

This is a brief introduction of all the other parts of the business plan. The overview describes your business and includes a sentence or two about its major aspects: the customer, the competition, the location, the financing needs.

You may want to go back and revise the overview after completing the rest of the business plan, but it is helpful to write an accurate description of your business before you start any other section. Try to do this in only one or two sentences. This I think of as preliminary acid test. Many people do not really understand what business they are in, or they make the business more expansive than it should be. One major function of the business plan, in fact, is to target your market as much as possible, because a small, narrowly defined business invariably does better than a larger, more amorphous one.

Over the years in my small-business classes, I've met many people who want to start a restaurant that will also sell antiques (usually the table and chairs customers sit on) and perhaps incorporate a T-shirt stand as well. While I applaud the energy that goes into this kind of thinking, more often than not such businesses are doomed. Most of us simply cannot be everything to everyone, at least not very well, but we can do one thing very well. It's a good point to keep in mind when planning any kind of freelance business. Keep it small, at least initially, and target, target, target. Remember, you can always expand when the business does well. But it is much harder to downsize successfully, as some very big American businesses have recently learned the hard way.

So the first step in writing a business plan is to submit your idea to the acid test. Describe your business briefly. If you cannot do this, you do not know what business you are starting, or you have not targeted the business enough. If you can do it, you are ready to move on to the rest of the business plan.

CUSTOMER PROFILE

A business guru once wrote that the single most important element of any business is the customer. Interestingly, lots of entrepreneurs dispute this fact. They believe that the force of their personality, their talent, or their skill will bring them customers. But businesses do not work like this. Instead, you must offer a service that people want or need, and then they will begin to pay you money for it. Trying to sell people something they do not want or need, like trying to sell through the sheer force of your personality, often leaves you talking to an empty room—or store or studio. So the first thing you must do in a business plan is to figure out if there are potential customers who want to buy what you are selling. To do this, you research and write a customer profile.

This should contain the following information:

- Customer's age. This is the single most important piece of information you can know about your customer. We all buy different services and goods depending on our ages. Teens do not buy what young marrieds buy, and young marrieds do not buy what empty nesters buy. Much, if not everything, depends on how old your customers are.
- Income. This tells you one important fact: Can your potential customer afford to buy your service? If you are planning to earn a living translating foreign-language books into English, you

need to know which publishers can afford to spend money on translation. Some consider this an important element of publishing, while others pay little attention to it. If you are a studio potter, you need to know that your potential customers can afford to buy your work. The business will fail if you charge museum prices before you have museum clients.

Cynthia should have paid a lot of attention to this vital fact. In a community of 50,000, there might not have been enough two-career parents to support a second, let alone a third, preschool, and this would have been an important and very basic detail for her to discover early in her research.

In addition to knowing your customers' income, it may be important to know their disposable income, especially if you are selling a luxury or nonessential service. Disposable income is what people have left over after they pay for life's necessities, such as rent, utilities, and food.

- Sex. Most simply put, women don't buy what men buy, and knowing your customer's sex is important for this reason. Jack, a magazine illustrator, decided to tap into the magazine market. Because he had just resigned a job with one, he initially targeted business magazines. Yet his designs had a decidedly soft edge to them. Since he was not interested in changing his basic style, Jack soon discovered that his true market was certain women's magazines, whose editors found his work stunning.

- Buying habits. A key thing to figure out about customers is how they will buy from you, because this often determines such important aspects of your business as the hours you are open, where you locate, and whether you must offer credit. It is important to obtain information on customers' buying habits, but you must also personalize this to your situation. Once you know, for example, that people who buy your service tend to buy regularly, two or three times a month, then you must ask yourself if this is true of your clientele as well.

Buying habits also determine what subsidiary services you must offer. Henrietta Johnson, a successful dog walker on the Upper West Side of Manhattan, found that she often gave her clients advice about their animals' personalities. After all, she observed the behavior of far more dogs over an extended time period than the average dog owner, or for that matter, most veterinarians, and she was an intuitive judge of animal behavior. This was information she dispensed free because she liked talking to her clients, but she might well have decided to charge for it. As a kind of subsidiary service, many of her clients would have paid for a consultation about their dog's personality, behavioral traits, and problems.

Most subsidiary services are more routine than this, involving such issues as whether you will provide pickup and delivery or extend credit to your customers, but every freelancer has to decide which ones are needed, whether to offer them, and whether to charge for them.

The customer profile should detail every aspect of your customers from how much they will spend to how they will get to you to how often they will buy from you and why. With this information, you can begin to make decisions about such things as how many customers you will need to draw, how you will be paid for your services, and what subsidiary services you have to offer. The customer profile is the most detailed section of most business plans and well worth the time and research it requires.

COMPETITORS' PROFILE

You need to examine the competition to see what you can do differently and, you hope, better. It is, however, not always necessary to do something better in order to succeed. If it were, you would never see four gas stations, all virtually identical, on the four corners of most freeway exits. In fact, in examining the competition, remember that you need to figure out not only what if anything will set you apart from your rivals but also and equally important what you must do that is exactly the same as your competitors.

In most freelance operations, the competition is local. Rarely will you need to examine competition that is not. In addition, don't get caught up examining peripheral businesses that do not do exactly what you do, unless you have no choice. Since many freelance businesses are somewhat esoteric, sometimes it is impossible to gather information on the exact business you want to start. In cases like this, look to other, similar businesses as you do your research and gather information on competitors. For example, furniture conservators would not find a lot of information on their area, a small specialty, but virtually all the information that applies to antique dealers also applies to furniture restorers. The two businesses move in tandem, in terms of the customers they attract, even in terms of how they respond to the economy. Anything a prospective restorer could find out about the antique business would be at least somewhat applicable to a restoration studio.

A complete competitor's profile should examine three to four direct, serious competitors. Here are some questions to ask and answer regarding the competition:

- How long has the competition been in business? Longevity is important because it builds customer loyalty. You may be able slowly to make a dent in a competitor's business, but you must be prepared to wait—and that takes more start-up money.
- How are their services the same as or different from yours? This is a key to examining the competition and also to shaping your business. Think about what you can or must do to set your business apart from the competition. Think about the ways it would be unwise to set yourself apart from them.
- What do they charge? Within reason you will have to charge approximately the same, but it may be possible, depending on your level of quality or the extra services you will provide, to charge more. You also may want to charge less and use price as a competitive tool. If the latter is your goal, though, you will probably have to cut some corners that your competition does not. One purpose of the competitors' profile is to figure out where those corners are and whether it's worthwhile to cut them.
- Who are your competitors' suppliers? This can provide leads to

suppliers you will use. Sometimes you will use exactly the same supplier; sometimes you will need to find new ones in order to better the competition.

- Who are your competitors' customers? The presumption is that you will be seeking the same customers, but occasionally you will discover that you want to reach out to a higher- or lower-end customer. This is fine-tuning at its best.
- What are the competitors' strengths and weaknesses? This is what allows you to say that you can do something better than the competition. After gathering as much information as you can about your competitors, analyze this very carefully.

How exactly are you supposed to figure out what the competition is up to? You may be able to make firsthand observations by hanging out in their place of business or even by working for a while in a competitor's employment. Talk to people who use the competition. Tell them you're thinking about starting a similar business and ask them what the competition is or is not doing for them.

More general information is also available in trade magazines and journals, which publish financial statistics about their industries several times a year. This information often includes such vital facts as average earnings and profits of businesses, as well as areas of strong and weak sales.

After you assess the competition, you must ask yourself whether there is room for one more business like it. If there is, continue working on your business plan to shape your idea more fully. But if you conclude that there is not room for any more competition, then it may be time to go to plan B, your backup business idea.

SALES FORECAST

This is one of the trickier parts of any business plan. Based on what you have learned about the customer and the competition, you must make an estimate—or a guesstimate, as some people call it—of your projected sales.

It is important not to guess too high or too low. If your estimate is too optimistic, you will believe you have a better chance of succeeding in this business than you actually do. If you are too pessimistic, you will aim too low and may never realize your full potential.

The sales forecast marks a turning point in planning your business. If you determine that you can indeed earn a living plus the profit you will need to keep this business afloat, then you are ready to move ahead with the business plan.

If your conclusion is that this is not a business that will permit you to earn a decent living, let alone a profit, then reject this idea and begin to look for another business to start.

LOCATION

If the happy news is that your business still looks like a go, the next step is to think about where you will locate. Many freelancers are home-based. Unfortunately, this leads some people to conclude, erroneously, that no planning is required. They imagine they will simply shove the dinner table aside and move in a desk, or maybe even start using the dinner table as their desk. But if you really want your home-based business to take off, you will put considerable time and effort into planning its physical layout. Contact an interior designer whose specialty is designing a home-based business or work with a store designer who sells contract (business) furniture.

If you will be opening an office outside your home, your first consideration is whether you need to be located somewhere special. A Chicago off-line editor who did work for advertising agencies did his research and accurately concluded that he had to be located within a few blocks of the major advertising agencies. Not only would they not travel to his suburban home (which would have enabled him to operate very inexpensively), but they would not travel more than a few blocks. When he located office space two blocks from four major advertising agencies, two of whom were already clients, he did a lot to ensure the success of his business.

ORGANIZATIONAL PLAN

Ah, the proverbial organizational plan. In a major corporation, this consists of a highly detailed flowchart. In a small freelance operation where you are the CEO, the sales staff, the cleaning person, and the accountant, there is little need to draw such a chart to remind you of exactly how much work you will be doing in the next few years.

What may be helpful is to draw up a list of all the responsibilities and functions of the business—bookkeeping, sales, cleaning, creating new products, ordering supplies, etc. Then study the list carefully to see what is possible. In the course of doing this, you may discover your own strengths and weaknesses. You also may discover that you need to hire an employee, whether you want to or not.

At this point, your strengths are not as important as your weaknesses. If you will be the chief bookkeeper but have never been able to balance your personal checkbook, you may need take some action to improve your bookkeeping skills. Consider taking an accounting or business math course. You could also hire a part-time bookkeeper to help you out. Even if you do not keep your own financial books, though, you need to know enough to be able to read them. I suggest that all freelancers make sure they have some familiarity with basic bookkeeping for a business before they start any endeavor.

Similarly, if you see so much work ahead of you that you cannot imagine taking a day off, let alone going on vacation for the next three years, then this business may be too big for one person to operate. Certainly Cynthia would have discovered this fact had she investigated the preschool more carefully before opening her doors. If this is the case, you may have a few months' leeway before you must hire someone, but you know that this is something you must plan for in your immediate future.

MARKETING PLAN

Closely tied to the customer profile is the marketing plan. This is where you plan how you will attract the customers you described earlier.

Customers will come to you because of your price, your service, and your advertising. In the marketing plan, you describe how you will handle all three of these areas or at least the ones that apply to your operation. All businesses set prices, but not all freelance operations have a need for customer service policies or advertising.

Unfortunately, pricing is an inexact science. By now, though, you should know what your competition charges and should have analyzed whether you can go higher or whether you must go lower or stay the same.

There are many components to the quality of the service you provide, but for most freelancers, service policies revolve around two things: your payment policies and any subsidiary services you have to offer. Will you be paid immediately on rendering your services, or will you give your clients a grace period of anywhere from two weeks to a month for payment? Will you need to provide credit? If so, accepting credit cards (few businesses bother with house accounts anymore) costs you money. Most cards charge between 4 and 9 percent, so take this figure into account in your financial planning.

Will you go to your customers, or will they come to you? Will you need to hire messengers or use mail services? All this must be calculated into the cost of doing business, so what you decide about these aspects of your operation matters.

As the last step in a marketing plan, you must figure out how you will make prospective customers aware of your services. Freelancers rarely can afford to mount full-scale advertising campaigns, nor are these necessary or particularly effective for a small business. Instead, they rely on a host of other proven methods of advertising. Effective methods include direct mail, telephone solicitation, flyers, publicity, and advertisements in the trade press or small publications.

FINANCIAL PLAN

For most businesses the financial plan is the heart and soul of the business plan. It typically takes up as much space as all the other minireports combined and usually includes a profit-and-loss statement, a balance sheet, and one to three years of projected budgets. For freelancers, the financial plan is a simpler affair but an important one nevertheless.

If you are unlikely to qualify for a bank loan because of the size and scope of your business, you need not bother with a profit-and-loss statement or a balance sheet. Instead, the following pages contain some financial tools that are not usually included in a business plan but that work especially well for a freelance operation. These will give you a more complete financial picture of the business you plan to start.

The goal of a financial plan is to show you whether you have enough money to start the business and operate it for six months to a year—the length of time it takes most businesses to show any kind of profit. Because so many freelancers tend to merge their personal and businesses lives, you will get a more complete financial picture if you calculate your living expenses in addition to the costs related to the business at least during the first year or so of operation. Most prospective freelancers need to see not only if they can afford to start and operate a business but also whether they can survive while they do so.

Personal Expenses

The best place to start is with your personal expenses, which must be met every month. Also, you will probably use your own cash to support your freelance venture for a few months at least. Thus, you need to figure out how much money you have and how much is needed to meet your monthly expenses. If need be, keep a running record over several months to get an accurate estimate of what you spend. The charts on pages 30 and 31 will help you determine this.

Estimate your expenses in each category. Then examine them carefully. Is there anything you can cut back? For example, you will no longer have to eat lunch out every day, nor will you have to maintain a wardrobe for work if you have a home office. Your commuting expenses will be far less. Can you go without a vacation for a year or

RESOURCES FOR STARTING A BUSINESS

	Monthly	Annually

Savings account
Pension (Will you get anything
  when you leave your
  present employer?)
Dividends, interest (from stocks,
  money funds, etc.)
Gifts and bonuses or vacation
  pay to which you may be
  entitled when you resign
Unemployment (if you are
  eligible)
Wages from job assignments or
  part-time job		

two? Be realistic about what you can or cannot live without. Everyone has a personal limit for sacrifice, and you will be miserable if you do not recognize yours.

Business Expenses

The next step is to project your business expenses. When you are starting a freelance business, your projected expenses will fall into two categories: start-up costs and operational expenses. The former occur only once; the latter must be met month after month as you freelance.

The chart on page 33 lists one-time start-up costs and helps you plan how to meet these expenses. Start by including every possible cost you might have to meet and every possible furnishing you might want to buy. Later, you can go back and revise this chart, based on what you actually will be able to spend. At that point, set up a list of future purchases you would like to make as you become more prosperous and secure. The chart on page 34 outlines your monthly business expenses.

ESTIMATED MONTHLY LIVING EXPENSES
(personal)

	First Month	Second Month	Third Month
Housing (rent or mortgage)			
Utilities			
Phone			
Food			
At home			
In restaurants			
Insurance			
Homeowner's and renter's			
Medical, which you must			
now pay in entirety			
Medical and dental			
Loan repayments or debts			
Savings account (yes, you			
should still maintain one)			
Special savings fund (for			
purchases such as home			
upkeep and furniture,			
clothes)			
Transportation			
Entertainment			
Vacations			
Child care			
Miscellaneous expenses			
Inflation factor (add 10 percent)			
TOTAL PROJECTED EXPENSES			

Now add your start-up costs and your estimated monthly living and business expenses for at least the first few months to see if you have enough money to start the freelance business. These expenses vary so much, depending on the kind of business you are starting and such things as whether you will maintain a home office, that there is no accurate way to determine how much money any one freelancer might need. To be on the safe side, though, regardless of what kind of freelance business you are starting, you should try to have an amount equal to what you will need to live on and to run the business on for at least six months, preferably a year.

There are exceptions, of course. If you resign your full-time job but still have a trust or income from dividends that will allow you to support yourself, you have few worries. More realistically, if you have already landed a huge freelance job that begins the day after you put the finishing touches on your office and that runs for six months to a year, then you may feel comfortable reducing the amount of backup capital you will need. But remember that eventually that job will run out or you may hit a dry spell, and you must be prepared for this. Every freelancer needs a sizable emergency fund to tide him or her over such periods—or even to use while job hunting if freelancing turns out not to suit you.

The calculations you have just done are important in terms of helping you decide whether you can afford to freelance at this time. You can always start on a shoestring, but there is one major disadvantage in doing that. In a business where most operations are started on very little, if you reduce the amount still more, you may never catch up. You run the risk of always living hand-to-mouth.

The next step is to draw up a projected one- to three-year budget for the business. Include your projected income from sales even though it is only an estimate. These are very important forms that you will use over and over again.

You cannot review a budget too often when you are starting a new business, and even seasoned business owners review their budgets and goals quarterly if not monthly. At the end of your first year of operation, redo the second-year budget based on the current year's sales and expenses. You will now know, for example, when your slow and your peak seasons occur, and you will have an even more realistic sales forecast. Incorporate this into next year's budget.

Once you have completed the projected budgets, it is time to take a long, hard look at all the financial data to see whether you have the financial wherewithal to start a business. Line up all the information, especially the resources chart on page 30 and the start-up expenses chart on page 33, and compare this information to your sales fore-

START-UP COSTS

Item	If you plan to pay cash in full, enter the full amount below and in the last column	If you are going to pay by installments, fill out the columns below. Enter in the last column your down payment plus at least one installment.			Estimate the cash you need for furniture, fixtures, and equipment.
		Price	Amount of each installment	Down payment	
Furniture	$	$	$	$	$
Equipment:					
computer					
phone machine					
fax					
radio or television					
other					
Office supplies*					
Decorating and remodeling					
Utilities deposits					
Legal and accounting fees for setup					
Insurance*					
Professional fees and dues*					
Advertising and marketing for setup					
Operating capital					
Cash to live on while business gets going					
TOTALS	$	$	$	$	$

*These are ongoing expenses, but they must be included in setup costs because you will need money to finance them initially.

ESTIMATED MONTHLY BUSINESS EXPENSES

Item	Estimated Cost
Your salary (what you need to live on per month)	
Salaries and wages of persons whom you subcontract to work for you	
Rent for office	
Advertising	
Phone answering service	
Other utilities	
Messenger and other services	
Office supplies	
Other professional supplies	
Insurance	
Taxes and social security	
Legal and accounting fees	
Transportation	
Entertainment	
Professional memberships	
Repayment of loans	
Miscellaneous	
TOTAL	

cast. (You should now be able to see how important it is to make a realistic projection of your sales.) Ask yourself one very important question: Do you have the money to start and operate this business until the business becomes self-supporting? If the answer is yes, your idea is a good one and you should go on to the next stage of planning. If the answer is no, then you need to rethink the plan, but all may not be lost. In a sense, this is a starting point. It is where you begin playing with the figures to see if you can make them work.

In order to salvage the idea you have for a business, you will probably have to do one of four things.

Obtain outside financing. This may mean a bank loan, but there are other ways to finance a business. Can a family member or friend lend you money? Can you find a backer who is willing to invest in your business? Some freelancers pay off their credit card loans and use this line of credit when they need to. Others take out a home equity loan and use that to fund their new business.

If a loan is out of the question, you still have three options.

Charge more for your services. Most new—and even many established—freelancers have a tendency to underprice themselves. This can skew your financial plans and make an otherwise viable business look like a losing proposition. Carefully look over your entire business plan, paying special attention to your financial figures, to see whether you fall into this category. Since the price we set on our services often involves issues of self-esteem, you might also solicit some respected outside advice, someone who will really level with you about your prospects for operating a successful business. Ask a friend or an adviser at the Small Business Administration or a university's small-business center to look over your business plan and talk to you about it. It's not so hard to ask for advice. The really hard part is listening to it and then acting on it.

Sell more. This may or may not be possible, but again review your business plan. Have you been too conservative in estimating your sales? Could you sell more if you hired an assistant or a salesperson? Don't just decide to sell more (that's too easy), but instead look in every nook and cranny of your business plan for some concrete fact or indication that you can actually sell more.

Start a more modest business. This is the path most freelancers end up taking, for a very good reason. Far too many people envision themselves running a more complex business than they need to in order to be successful. Remember the example of the entrepreneur who wanted to run a restaurant–antique store–T-shirt stand? If you are a grandiose planner, it's time to take a step back and make some more realistic plans. Put your obvious creativity to work elsewhere, in a smaller, more scaled-down business.

For a few people, there will not be a last-minute save. Your business idea does not fly. It is not, unfortunately, a good business to start. Ideally, this is something to discover at a much earlier stage of researching and writing the business plan, usually around the time that you prepare a sales forecast, which in turn is based on the customer and competitors' profiles. A few unlucky souls will not discover that their idea does not work until they do the financial plan, although to be truthful, the signs were probably there all along, and they chose to ignore them.

When this happens, there is only one thing to do: admit this is not a business that you can start at this time and hope to make successful. Unhappy as this discovery may be, it is better to find this out on paper, as you just did, than to throw your mother's IRA money, your kid's college fund, your personal savings—and your sanity—at a losing proposition.

As for the business plan you spent the better part of the last three months researching and writing, well, in the heart of most prospective freelancers, there usually lurks more than one good business idea. Consider this business plan a trial run, a test of your managerial abilities. Take a breather and then get to work on the next idea.

Most people, though, if they have done their homework, discover at the completion of their business plan that with a few modifications, their idea is a good one. The next step is to begin preparations to open the business.

3

CHOOSING A LEGAL STRUCTURE

ONCE YOU HAVE GIVEN THE GREEN LIGHT to your idea for a freelance business, the next step is to research the kind of legal structure that works best for you. An unincorporated sole proprietorship meets the needs of the vast majority of freelancers, but it is helpful to know about other kinds of legal structures as well. Yours may be the exceptional business that will fare better under another umbrella. Then, too, some businesses start out with one legal format and then move on to something else as the business grows or changes direction. Since it is not always easy or even permitted to move from one legal structure to another, it is important to figure out where you want to start as well as where you might end up.

The legal structure of a business affects the amount of taxes it pays and the degree of liability to which the owner is subject should he or she default on a loan or find himself or herself in the midst of a lawsuit. Both an accountant and a lawyer are helpful in reaching any decision about how to organize a business legally.

The three basic forms of business ownership, from the least regulated to the most, are:

- Sole proprietorship
- Corporation
- Partnership

SOLE PROPRIETORSHIP

A sole proprietorship is wholly owned—and typically managed as well—by one person. It is the simplest and least expensive form of legal organization, which may account for the fact that more than 70 percent of the nation's small businesses opt for this type of ownership.

It is the least regulated and the least expensive form of legal organization. In contrast to a partnership and a corporation, there are no federal or state forms or papers to file when you organize a sole proprietorship. You simply hang out your shingle—or more likely, plug in your computer—and declare yourself open for business.

Depending on the kind of freelance business you are setting up, though, you may be required to obtain various city and/or state licenses. If you choose to do business under a name other than your own, for example, in most states and cities you must file a Doing Business As form (called a DBA) so the state knows who is operating the business. This means that if you call your business the Evergreen Editorial Services instead of Suzanne Jones (your name), then you must file a DBA. The best way to learn about these and other local and regional legal requirements is to contact the state, county, and city in which you will be conducting business for a packet of information on operating a small business. The IRS also offers a free packet of information about legal structures of businesses.

A sole proprietorship, like any legal structure, offers advantages and disadvantages. All the decisions, for example, will be made by you, for better or for worse. If you are truly an independent soul, you will thrive on this. But if you are more of a team player, the person who always organizes the carpool or the tenants' committee, then you may feel burdened by a sole proprietorship. In addition to getting to make all the decisions, you get all the responsibility. Some people flourish in this situation while others wilt.

The tax situation of a sole proprietor is relatively straightforward. There are no business taxes per se on sole proprietorships. All the money in the business flows through to you, and you pay taxes on your income as an individual. You are, however, allowed to take numerous business-related deductions, which you declare on a tax form called a Schedule C (Profit or Loss in a Business or Profession). This is filed along with the standard 1040 tax form that all taxpaying citizens use. (See Chapter 8 on taxes, though, because businesses do pay taxes at different times from individuals.)

Some deductions that are available to other legal structures are denied to sole proprietorships. You cannot, for example, deduct your own salary unless you are incorporated. You can deduct only a portion of your health insurance. For many years sole proprietors could not deduct any Social Security, even though corporations were allowed to deduct the portion they paid for their employees. Now sole proprietors can deduct a portion of their Social Security as well.

A sole proprietorship also affects the freelance business's legal liability. In an unincorporated sole proprietorship, you are liable for any debts of the business. This means that you personally can be sued to satisfy any debts of the business. Anyone who sues you, in fact, not just lenders, can make a claim against your personal assets.

This is the sticking point that causes many inexperienced business planners to begin to think they had better incorporate. But a closer look at the situation usually reveals that incorporation is still unnecessary—or worse, not truly protective.

Ask yourself, for example, exactly what liabilities you expect to encounter as you operate your business. A freelance editor who works at home and meets clients in their offices does not really need much if any liability protection. No client or business associate is going to bring a lawsuit after slipping on an icy walk in front of the house or tripping over Grandma's oriental rug in the foyer. But a freelance photographer who stretches electric wires and other equipment across city streets while doing a photographic shoot may be in another position entirely. This person may indeed need some liability protection.

But before rushing to incorporate, it pays to take a closer look at your situation. Have others in your circumstances incorporated, or do they carry liability insurance, perhaps a kind that can be purchased on a situation-by-situation basis? Does the film company that hires you provide liability insurance? Once you do determine that you need liability protection of this sort, ask yourself if incorporation is the only way to obtain it, or if there is another, less expensive way to acquire it. Perhaps you belong to a professional group that offers some form of liability insurance. Any other means is ultimately likely to be cheaper and simpler than incorporation.

There is another form of liability you are more likely to encounter. It involves the following scenario. You fail to repay a loan. The lender sues, and if you are unincorporated, he or she goes after your personal as well as your business assets. We'd all like protection from this, but incorporation may not be the answer. First, consider whether in fact you have any personal assets worth seizing. If you do not, then it is not worth your while to pay the costs of incorporating in order to protect assets you do not have. Second, most savvy lenders, that is, bankers, now see through this ruse of incorporation, at least where very small businesses are involved. These days, many lenders ask lendees to sign a waiver of liability, which means, in effect, that they can still seize any personal assets if you default on the loan.

For these reasons it is usually not worthwhile for a freelancer to incorporate. But each business is different, and this decision should be made by you, your lawyer, and your accountant.

Many freelancers begin with a sole proprietorship and then, when their business takes off, switch to another legal structure. It is easier to move from a sole proprietorship to a corporation than it is to move in the opposite direction. For example, those who form S corporations, a spinoff form of incorporation that appeals to many freelancers (more on these below), are barred from forming another S corporation for five years after disbanding one. Thus it behooves any freelancer to carefully weigh from the beginning which form of business ownership will work best for him or her, as well as which form you might want to move into if the business grows in such a way as to make this necessary.

CORPORATION

A corporation is an artificial legal structure that has most (but not all) of the rights of an individual. Supreme Court Justice John Marshall in 1819 described this remarkable legal structure as "an artificial being, invisible, intangible, and existing only in contemplation of law."

Corporations can buy and own other businesses, buildings, or other forms of property; sign contracts; sue and be sued; and conduct a host of other business activities just as individuals can.

In the United States, businesses usually incorporate in the state in which their headquarters are located, although it is possible to live and operate a business in one state and be incorporated in another. (The reason for doing this is to save money; some states tax corporations more heavily than others.)

Corporations issue stock, and its owners are shareholders. A corporation may be either public or private. In a public corporation, stock is bought and sold publicly, while in a privately held corporation—the kind that virtually all freelancers form—the owner or his or her family owns all the stock.

From the moment of inception, corporations are the most highly regulated form of legal organization. Before a state permits a corporation to be formed, it requires that certain information be filed. There is also a host of other forms and reports that corporations must file with the state throughout their existences. In fact, one very sensible reason for a freelancer not to incorporate is to avoid the added paperwork, which is considerable. Corporations also must identify themselves by using Inc., Co., or Ltd. in their names.

Technically it is possible to incorporate yourself. You will save money by doing this, and there are several books that will walk you through the necessary steps. Incorporation, though, is almost never a simple process, so even if you decide to do much of the legwork yourself, you should still seek expert advice about whether this is really the most suitable form of legal structure for you.

A tax preparer's or accountant's advice is especially important since incorporation changes your tax picture in significant ways. Corporations are subject to a variety of federal, state, and local taxes. Other taxes—the excess earnings tax, to name just one—apply to some corporations in certain circumstances.

You will also be taxed on the dividends that are paid to you as a shareholder of the corporation as well as on your personal earnings. This is the "double taxation" of corporations. As an unincorporated sole proprietor, you pay taxes once, on your income from the business. For a freelancer the added taxes are often the major drawback to incorporation.

Both the federal and state governments have shown a tendency to tax corporations more readily than individuals on grounds that any tax increase will be passed along in the price of the product, but for those who run a service-oriented freelance business, it is not always possible to pass along the extra tax burden.

As a very general rule of thumb, it is usually beneficial for a freelancer to incorporate only when corporate taxes are considerably lower than personal income taxes. Not too many years ago, for example, the top personal income tax bracket was 90 percent (the income tax scale was much more graduated then than it is now) while the top corporate tax hovered around 20 percent. Obviously this made incorporation very attractive to virtually any kind of business.

Since a major tax reform act was enacted in the late 1980s, though, the corporate tax rate has hovered at about 28 percent while individual tax rates have ranged from 28 to 35 percent. With these changes, it is much less advantageous for a business, especially a small freelance operation, to incorporate for tax purposes. Still, this is a decision you have to make with your accountant based on your individual circumstances.

The other major reason to incorporate is liability protection. When a corporation is sued by a discontented customer, the personal assets of the owner are typically not at risk. But as was noted in the earlier discussion about sole proprietorships, if you have no assets to protect, then it makes little sense to incorporate. And if you are an incorporated freelancer taking out a business loan, you may be asked to sign a waiver that will put your personal assets at risk should you default.

As you learn about the pros and cons of incorporation, you may hear that it will be easier to sell your freelance business if you incorporate. But this, too, is more often than not a false promise for the freelancer. Most freelance operations *are* the owner's talent, and the owner's talent is the business, the entire business. Therefore, any freelance business is tricky if not impossible to sell, whether or not it is incorporated.

While corporations can add to your tax burden, they also provide some tax savings. If you are incorporated, for example, you may deduct all your health insurance as well as your salary. You are entitled to establish a corporate pension fund, although the amount you can shelter in this vehicle is no more than can be sheltered in a Keogh.

However much fun it is to incorporate and be able to use Inc., Co., or Ltd. after your name (and I'm convinced that's why some people who shouldn't incorporate do so), it is also expensive, costing anywhere from several hundred to several thousand dollars, the latter being the more usual amount. For this and the other reasons described, it is important to weigh all the advantages and disadvantages of incorporation and consult with both an accountant and a lawyer before making any decision. An accountant or tax preparer will explore the tax ramifications with you, while a lawyer will help you decide whether to form a C corporation or one of the other variations on incorporation.

S Corporation

The S corporation is the most common form of specialized incorporation used by freelancers, often more useful than a C corporation. An S corporation is a pseudocorporation that offers its owners liability protection while still permitting them to be taxed as individuals. In other words, as an S corporation, you do not pay corporate taxes; rather, your income is taxed once as if you were an unincorporated sole proprietor.

S corporations are more closely regulated than unincorporated sole proprietorships but are not subject to the heavy regulation of a C corporation. (Still, your mail will increase greatly in volume the day that you form any kind of corporation.) There is much more paperwork with an S corporation than with a sole proprietorship. In addition, some taxes, such as worker's compensation, to which you will be subject as an S or C corporation, must be paid monthly, an unpleasant prospect for a freelancer with an erratic cash flow. (Businesses, incorporated or not, pay their federal taxes quarterly.)

While S corporations are a boon for some freelancers, they may not be any more of a panacea than a C corporation, nor do they offer any greater liability protection. Getting a loan will still be difficult, whether you form a C corporation, an S corporation, or remain an unincorporated sole proprietor.

An S corporation is subject to a host of restrictions. In general, they don't affect most freelance operations, but you should nevertheless know they exist. An S corporation can have no more than thirty-five owners, and none can be other corporations or non-U.S. citizens. No more than 20 percent of an S corporation's income may come from passive sources, such as rent, royalties, interest, or sale of stock. This can make it an unacceptable form of ownership, for example, for authors. If you disband an S corporation, you cannot organize another one for five years. Finally, although all S corporations are taxed only once federally, each state imposes its own taxes on S corporations. In some states, New York, for example, S corporations literally have been taxed out of existence in recent years.

PARTNERSHIP

A partnership is a form of legal organization in which two or more persons form a business, sharing, one hopes, both the responsibilities and the burdens of the endeavor.

Although most freelancers work alone, some do choose to have partners. Nancy Mazer and P. J. Fuller, two enterprising women who joined forces several years ago, are an excellent example of a free-lance partnership that works. Their business is also unusual in that it breaks one of the cardinal rules of freelancing, which is that you should, as much as possible, narrow the area or areas in which you offer services. Mazer and Fuller provide a range of services, from typing to helping people settle into a new city to finding an unusual birthday gift for someone. Part of their success is undoubtedly due to the fact that they were smart enough to team up with each other, an act that gave them more validity as a business than either would have had alone. As a solo act, either woman might have lacked the credibility because of the scattershot approach to the services they offer; together, they make it all work as a business.

If you think you might need or want a partner, here are some things to consider:

- Why do you need a partner? For the money? Experience? Moral support? All these are valid reasons, but you should be clear about which one(s) apply to you before you start a partnership. The reason for forming a partnership should be a subject of open discussion between you and any potential partners.
- What are the pros and cons of going it alone versus forming a partnership? It is not enough to admit that you are too scared to go it alone, since that still may be the best course of action for you. Before you form a partnership, think about the advantages and disadvantages; there will always be some of both.
- What do others in your field do? If few people form partnerships, there is probably a reason, and that is usually because there are too few financial advantages. If many people are partners, you can bet that there is a reason for that, too.

Advantages and Disadvantages of a Partnership

There are many kinds of partnerships, and if you are thinking of forming one, you should consult with a lawyer who can explain the possible arrangements to you. The differences among the various kinds of legal structures are also well explained in the Small Business Administration (SBA) pamphlet, "Selecting the Legal Structure for Your Firm," available free by writing SBA, P.O. Box 15434, Fort Worth, Texas 76119. Most freelancers seek active partners, that is, persons who will be full participants in the business, but some find partners who offer financial support and little else.

The advantages of a partnership are that it is easily formed and relatively free of government regulation and special taxation. It offers much the same flexibility of a sole proprietorship. As in the case of Mazer and Fuller, two persons acting together are often stronger than two persons acting individually, and a partnership offers such advantages as shared management and twice as much experience and skill as a sole proprietor would have. In certain cases, a partnership can obtain financing more easily than can a sole proprietorship.

The major disadvantage is that you must share your profits and your interest in the business. If your partner is active, you must take his or her views and management ideas into account. Furthermore, in a partnership, at least one partner must have unlimited liability such as a sole proprietor has. A partnership is unstable in that it is dissolved if one partner leaves the partnership or dies, although you can buy partnership insurance to cover this possibility. There also may be difficulties if one partner wants to buy the other one out; a way to avoid this is to write arrangements for executing this into the partnership contract.

Be aware that each partner can make legally binding contracts without the other partner's knowledge or consent. Once these contracts are formed, the other partners are subject to their terms. Because of this, it behooves anyone who forms a partnership to work out in advance the role that each partner will play. Responsibilities and duties should be spelled out as well in the partnership agreement.

Partnerships work best if each partner has his or her own areas of responsibility and if all areas that need tending to are covered by one or the other partner. Partnerships have been known to founder because there is one area that neither partner is willing to take responsibility for. Partnerships also collapse for the opposite reason. If you cannot delegate responsibility or give up some control, a partnership probably isn't right for you.

Partnership power can be divided in any number of ways. Some partnerships elect a general partner who runs the business for his or her term of office. Sometimes one person always tends to the business aspects of the operation while the partner is the creative force. Sometimes partners rotate responsibilities. Unfortunately, many partnerships operate in a haphazard manner, with no clearly defined areas of responsibility. Even in a small freelance partnership, it is always better to outline carefully each partner's duties and responsibilities. It is never a good idea to form a partnership without a written agreement that also describes the sharing of assets, profits, and losses as well. A lawyer can draw up such a contract.

Partnerships can be either incorporated or unincorporated. If they are incorporated, they pay taxes as a corporation and are afforded the same liability protection. Partners in an unincorporated partnership pay taxes as individuals, although the partnership is required to file an information-only return. Unincorporated partnerships are more closely regulated than unincorporated sole proprietorships, less so than corporations.

Limited Liability Company

As with corporations, there are several variations on partnerships. One that is gaining in popularity with freelancers is the fairly new legal structure known as a limited liability company (LLC). This is something like an S corporation for partnerships. As is the case with an S corporation, profits are taxed only once, when you pay taxes as an individual. And also like an S or a C corporation, the LLC offers some limited protection from liability.

An LLC offers enough advantages so that in states where S corporations have been taxed out of existence, some freelancers are forming LLCs, using a spouse as co-owner of the business as a partner.

The biggest disadvantage of LLCs as of this writing is that they are still new and thus relatively untested legally. The laws regulating them are not yet consistent from state to state, nor are they fully established. As more LLCs are formed, litigation will undoubtedly resolve many of the questions that now surround them. Like an S corporation, there are some restrictions on health insurance deductions for LLCs. Disbanding an LLC can also trigger some taxes, something to be weighed before opting for this organization.

The cost of organizing an LLC is comparable to the cost of forming a corporation. Since this is in addition to a partnership agreement, these are not inexpensive organizations to form. Despite these disadvantages, LLCs are an interesting, helpful legal entity with special appeal for freelancers.

GETTING EXPERT ADVICE

Finally, while this chapter covers the most commonly used legal structures, there is much more to be learned before choosing one. As noted throughout this chapter, no one should choose a legal structure without consulting, first an accountant and then a lawyer. Of these two, the accountant's opinion probably should carry the most weight. A lawyer is helpful for drawing up any papers and for pulling together the appropriate forms, but only an accountant can help you decide which form of legal organization will provide you with the greatest tax savings. And ultimately this is the major reason that freelancers choose one form of legal organization over another.

4

SETTING UP AN OFFICE

ORGANIZING YOUR PHYSICAL SPACE CAN BE THE most exhilarating part of starting a freelance business. It is the time when you begin to see some tangible proof that everything you have been carefully planning is actually going to happen. And one of the nicer things about setting up a freelance office is that you can often do it on the cheap. Excluding technology, which is covered in the next chapter, the investment in your office can be as small or as large as you want—or need—it to be. Fortunately, how much you spend has little to do with the kind of environment you ultimately create for yourself. One enterprising freelancer created a broad work surface using wooden sawhorses, with doors as table- and desktops. Her file cabinets fit neatly under the doors, and she bought several secondhand bookcases and painted them bright blue.

If you will call on your clients, you can get away with investing very little in fixing up an office. On the other hand, if your clients will be meeting with you at your office, you may have to spend a bit more, but again, the amount you spend has little to do with the result if you're willing to do most of the labor yourself and look for secondhand office furniture.

PLANNING THE KIND OF OFFICE YOU NEED

Before you jump into planning an office, consider your needs very carefully. To start with, do you really need an office? If you are a consultant who will be working mostly in other people's offices, you may be able to get along, as one freelance wardrobe planner does, with a file cabinet in your linen closet and a shelf or two devoted to office supplies. On the other hand, if you are an artist, you will need considerably more space in which to work, although it probably will not be an office per se. Of more importance to you than where you can store supplies, for example, will be the kind of light you need to work by. Editors and others who work in publishing also require a lot of table space on which to spread out their projects and reference materials. Sooner or later most freelancers need an office, however, if only some kind of a cubbyhole in which to store a file cabinet.

After deciding that you need an office, the next important question is where to locate it. The answer depends on a combination of your personal and business needs. Judy, a freelance data processor, is also the mother of four small children. For her, there is no choice: "I maintain an office at home, because only there can I combine my two roles—mother and editor—most efficiently."

Many freelancers opt for a home office because they believe it is cheaper than an outside office and because they like the income tax deduction it gives them. Some freelancers do not even consider the alternative to having a home office. Sally Chapralis, a marketing and public relations consultant, says, "I maintain an office in my home. When I started freelancing, I assumed it was the only way to work, particularly in the economic sense. I wasn't knowledgeable or sophisticated enough to realize that there were other options. But it has worked out well enough."

Others do not so much plan for a home office as they let it emerge and gradually take over a part of their living spaces. This happened to Bryan Johnson, a freelance librarian: "I bought a computer for work. And I got filing cabinets. Then I got a table that is separate from my personal desk. It has no knickknacks—it's just for work. Now I've even rearranged my apartment since I'm so busy with the freelancing. My office is in a corner—near a window—where I can work without distraction."

Pros and Cons of a Home Office

There are decided pros and cons in having an office in your home, just as there are pros and cons to having an office outside your home. Here are some reasons to maintain a home office:

- The aforementioned tax deduction. You can deduct part of the rent or mortgage payment of your apartment or home. One word of caution here: You can deduct only the part of your mortgage that is not interest. If you have just bought a home and most of your monthly payment goes for interest, you may not be able to take a deduction for a home office as well. Since you already write off part of the interest, to deduct a home office on top of that would be a double tax break, something the IRS frowns on.
- There is usually no pressure to decorate, as there might be in an office outside your home.
- There is no commute to and from the office. This saves not only time but also money. You don't have to hassle with the weather, nor do you spend much on lunches, as you might be tempted to do if you worked in a business area or an office where you have others to lunch with.
- Your time is, in some respects, more flexible. You can go to work when you want to and take breaks when you want to. And you can run errands in your neighborhood anytime you wish.

Freelancers report the following disadvantages of a home office:

- Working at home can be lonely and stifling. Chuck, an editor who tried freelancing and found it wasn't to his liking, recalls his freelance days: "I didn't like working at home at all. I missed the personal contact, and I missed the office hustle and bustle." Even those who continue freelancing can experience this—

and they are the ones who need an office outside the home. Another freelancer reports: "I couldn't create at home. I had quit my job in anticipation of this highly creative life in my own space—*my* home office. After two weeks, I returned to my former employer, who was going to be my main client anyway, and asked for office space, which he gladly rented to me for a nominal fee. Now, seven years later, I still freelance, and I still have my cubbyhole in my ex-employer's office. He's still a client, but I also have lots of other clients."

- You can waste a lot of valuable time procrastinating in your home office. The sight of a dirty room, the temptation of a new book, a sudden urge to have homemade split pea soup for lunch all can become major distractions when you work at home.

- If you have a mortgage, you may find yourself facing a tax bill when you sell your house or apartment. The portion of your profit that is derived from your commercial venture will be subject to taxation. The key word here is *profit*. If you sell in a bad market and do not show a profit, you may not have to worry about this, but if you sell at a profit, you may find yourself facing a sizable—$10,000 for one freelancer—tax bill. The only way to deal with this is to seek the advice of your accountant for several years before you sell.

- Some freelancers report that they hustle less when they have only one rent to pay. One book indexer comments: "Let's face it, I know I can earn less money because I have my office in my home. I earn enough every month to pay the rent and my other bills and to give myself spending money. I'm thinking about sharing an office with someone else or several people who work in publishing. It would get me going—in more ways than one. But the first thing is I would have to earn that extra rent."

Pros and Cons of an Office Outside Your Home

There are also reasons to decide to maintain an office outside your home. A big one is the need for company while you work. One woman, who had been earning her living as a freelance magazine writer for ten years, started with an office at home and moved to an outside office as quickly as possible, an unusual move for a writer, since they usually thrive on the solitude. She reports: "I tried working at home and realized I simply could not handle it, or at least it did not feel right to me. It was a struggle to get out of bed, and even more of a struggle to get to work. I felt even worse than when I was struggling to get up and go to someone's office to a job I didn't particularly like. I explained my problem to a friend who worked for a publisher, and she helped me arrange to take space in her boss's office. That's where I've been ever since. It has worked out really well. Left to my own devices, I am something of a slow starter, and I don't get to the office much before ten. But once there, I'm a hard worker, and I rarely leave before six or seven. I'm usually the last one to leave—which is something of an office joke since I'm my own boss."

To many freelancers, an outside office feels more professional, especially if they have to meet with clients. If you plan to receive many clients, an office not only may work best outside your home or in a separate room, but it often has to be fancier than most home offices. An outside office also separates your professional and personal life in a way that a home office does not. For freelancers who tend to be workaholics, this can be another plus.

On the other hand, there are disadvantages in having an office outside your home:

- It costs more because you must pay a separate rent as well as separate utilities.
- You have some added expenses in setting up. At home you can work in a chair in the living room or at the dining room table, but an office outside your home won't be of much use to you until it is set up with a desk, telephone, and other office appurtenances that are necessary for you to conduct business.
- You will have to spend money on lunch and commuting and possibly on a work wardrobe as well.
- You may find that your work schedule is more rigid than when you work at home. The urge to work may well come over you at 11 P.M., but you aren't likely to get dressed and trek down to the

office at that hour. Most freelancers who maintain offices outside their homes report that they tend to work fairly regular hours—nine to five—while freelancers who work at home tend to work those hours and then some.

Of course, there is one big, often overlooked advantage to having an office outside your home. All the expenses are deductible as a business expense. If your home office occupies one of four rooms in your house, you can deduct one-fourth of your mortgage, electricity, etc., but if you maintain an outside office, *all* of these expenses are deductible.

OFFICE LOCATION

Ultimately, where your office is located becomes a personal as well as financial decision. Barbara Zimmerman advocates a home office for freelancers: "When you move out of a home office, you move into rent, electric bills, a business phone, and clothes, and you lose all the tax advantages of having an office at home. It's a large chunk of money to have an office outside your home. Also, I work irregular hours. And I have a very busy season in the summer. I often work until one in the morning, and I wouldn't do that in an office. I have a compulsion to get things done. I don't know whether it's good or bad, but it means that I need an office in my home."

On the other hand, Robyn Cones, a freelance masseuse, has had it both ways and feels more comfortable with an office outside her home, even though she now works at home so she can care for her small child. She thinks it helped her business, too: "It's better outside—for my clients, that is. Coming to a masseuse makes a person vulnerable. You come and take off all your clothes, and if it is in someone else's home, it makes you that much more vulnerable. If it is an office—however homelike it is—the client can make the place his or her own. My office is not sterile; I have lots of wood and plants, for example. But I think it is good for my clients to know that no one lives there. Now that I work in my bedroom, it's harder. But there is a corridor for clients to walk down, and once the stereo is on, they will, I hope, feel as if they are in a special place. I'm also having a Murphy bed built, so my clients don't look at my bed or feel as much as if they're in a bedroom."

One freelance artist's representative, who now works in an office in her home, thinks of getting out: "I do eventually want an office outside my home. I now store my portfolios, which weigh about forty pounds, at a small art studio near where I make calls. Eventually, I will probably be able to rent a space from them, and I will definitely do it as soon as I can afford it. This is too hard, working at home. I can see my office reflected in a mirror from my bed. I hate that."

What it all boils down to is that freelancers, depending on their personalities, decide whether they want to work in or out of their homes. For those who do not want to work at home, even the benefit of a tax deduction does not carry much weight. And for those without much money who cannot stand to live and work in the same place, there are always deals to be negotiated, space to be traded for business favors, ways to band together with others in a similar situation. The important thing to remember is that you can always try one thing, and if that doesn't work, then you can do something else.

What to Look for in an Outside Office

If you want an office outside your home, the first step is to locate an adequate space for it. Before looking for office space, consider the following:

- How much space do you need to work in? Will a tiny corner do, or do you need a studio space? What kind of storage space do you require?
- How fancy must your office be? Will you be the only person seeing it? Will clients come to your office? If so, will they drop by for a few minutes, or will you need to have lengthy meetings there with them?
- What, if any, special features, do you need? Must the lighting

be natural or artificial? Is there enough wiring for your technology needs? Do you need any special temperature? Special ventilation? Make a list of all these special needs before you look at office spaces.

- What kind of location do you need? Do you want to be close to your home? To your clients? Do you need access to a messenger service?

What to Look for in a Home Office

When you start sizing up your home for a corner or room that would make a nice office, keep these things in mind:

- Is there enough storage space or enough room so you can build in what you need?
- Can the office accommodate your technology? The copy machine and scanner? The phone system? Your computer and printer?

Finally, consider whether the place where you hope to have your office is zoned for business. This is no problem in apartments in large cities such as Chicago and New York, but in the suburbs and in small towns, some residential areas do not permit businesses. If this is the case, and your neighbors are touchy on this point, they probably will tell you only after you have established an office. If, like most freelancers, you keep your office low-key and do not advertise in any overt way, there may be no problems. However, if you have frequent deliveries or must have a sign or some other form of advertising, then you may find yourself running afoul of zoning regulations. Or you may have trouble just because your neighbors don't like the idea of a business in a residential neighborhood.

To find out whether your prospective office site is zoned for business, contact the local zoning office. Better yet, pay them a visit. While you're there, you can check to see if any noisy or otherwise obtrusive construction is planned during the time you hope to stay in the office.

Leases and Office Space

If you plan to have your office in your home, no adjustments need be made to your lease, although if you are looking for an apartment and know you may start freelancing during the term of the lease, it may be best not to announce your business plans to any prospective landlords. In some cities more than one freelancer has found the rent taking a sudden jump when the landlord discovered that the apartment was also to be used as a place of business.

Once you've signed a lease, this is no problem, and you can quietly begin your freelance operation. Of course, if you already freelance full-time and are getting a new apartment, then your landlord will have to be told what you do for a living. Play it down, if possible, so you don't invite an increase in rent or too many questions.

Before you sign a lease for an office outside your home, there are a few things you need to know. Commercial rent is usually based on square feet of space. Business leases tend to run longer than domestic leases, but often there are no set rules about the length of the lease. This is frequently a negotiable point—to your advantage. For example, if you want a six-month lease, you might be able to get it for office space, or you might be able to get a five-year lease. Be sure that the lease runs for a period of time that suits you—whether it is only for a few months or a few years. And if possible get an option to renew for several years. Landlords will often do reconstruction to suit your needs in a commercial space. If you need such provisions, be sure the lease specifies *in writing* what remodeling or reconstruction work is to be done. If you are going to do the work yourself, this fact also should be mentioned in the lease.

Whether you work at home or in an outside office, it is incumbent upon you to be careful about any environmental hazards you may be posing on yourself and others. If you create noxious fumes, for example, or make a lot of noise, you need to find a space where this is acceptable or at least fixable. You will create problems for yourself if you take a space that does not accommodate your needs, or if you take a space and fail to make it environmentally sound.

FURNISHING AN OFFICE

The special needs and supplies of artists and craftpersons and others who need studio space are too diverse to describe here, and besides, those people know what their special requirements are. What the following pages do describe in detail are the supplies and office equipment you need to set up an efficient business office.

When you think about shopping for furniture for your office, consider whether you want—or can afford—to decorate or whether your office will be makeshift at first. There is nothing wrong with a makeshift office put together over several months or even years. In fact, this is often the best kind because such an office will emerge as a highly usable workspace suited exactly to your personal needs.

If you do not have a lot of money to spend, consider buying secondhand furniture. One freelance writer based in Manhattan haunted the secondhand office furniture shops near Canal Street and ended up with an office reminiscent of an earlier age. He found some old wooden file cabinets that were inexpensive yet very well built. You could not buy cabinets so well built in most furniture stores today. His large partners' desk (no, he doesn't have a partner, but he occasionally works as a freelance editor and claims he uses a different side of the desk for each activity) would cost thousands of dollars if he tried to buy either a new or an antique version in good condition; he got it for $350 and restored it himself. Secondhand office furniture stores specialize in perfectly usable, modern secondhand furniture, but they also frequently have items that are both funky and cheap as well as old, period furniture. Don't expect to find top-of-the-line, very expensive, or custom-made furniture in this market. You can buy furniture in good condition, and if you are willing to refinish and paint yourself, you can get some genuine bargains.

The next level up in furniture is, economically speaking, contract, or office, furniture. Office furniture is often very well built and for some reason less expensive in many instances than furniture designed for home use.

Many home-based freelancers prefer an office that looks more domestic than businesslike. They even succumb to furniture that is designed for home use rather than office use—a mistake in most instances. Not only is this the most expensive way to furnish a home office, but it is often inefficient and uncomfortable. Desks designed for home use, for example, are usually not as deep or as efficiently styled as desks designed for business use. This is not important if you sit at your desk once a month to pay bills, but if you work there long hours each day, the comfort of a desk becomes very important.

People who still want homey furniture in their offices can investigate home-furniture stores that offer a line of office furniture. Good sources are Crate & Barrel, IKEA, and Workbench, all of which also sell a line of office furniture that looks good in a home.

One freelance photo editor saved money and got exactly the office she wanted by buying a desk from Crate & Barrel and arranging for a carpenter to customize it for her. She got the workspace she needed and the look she wanted.

It is of the utmost importance to have an ergonomic office, that is, one that is kind to your body. Ergonomics experts know, for example, that a desk that is too low or high can cause physical discomfort. Keyboards that are not properly designed may contribute to carpal tunnel syndrome. Furthermore, the physical problems associated with a workspace that is not ergonomically designed often take years to develop, and by the time they do, they have already taken their toll on your body.

If you will be spending long hours at a computer or even at a desk, it may pay to hire the services of an ergonomics specialist to help design your workspace. Even artists and others who work in studios rather than offices need to pay attention to ergonomics when designing a space. All too often, freelancers do not concern themselves with such issues until their bodies start to show signs of wear and tear.

Finally, if there is one piece of office furniture that is especially sensitive to ergonomics, it is the chair you sit in all day. Investing in a good chair is not a luxury. It is an absolute necessity for most freelancers.

Filling in the Small Items

In home decorating, accessories are usually little more than finishing touches—bibelots whose only purpose is to create the ambiance you want. In office design, however, these small decorative items are often very important and far more than simply decorative. The letter holder that sits on your desk, the container that holds your stationery, even your wastebasket must be not only attractive but also functional.

And once again, the issue is how to find items that serve both purposes. The same stores that sell homelike office furniture often have accessories that work well in home offices. Mail-order catalogs—Hold Everything is superb in this area—also offer a plethora of ideas for finishing an office efficiently and attractively.

Finally, it is also possible to rent office furniture on a short- or long-term basis. Furniture rental is usually inexpensive, and if you aren't eager to invest in furniture before you are sure your business will take off, this is an excellent way to furnish an office. Get several estimates before you rent anything; prices vary from community to community and also from store to store.

SHOPPING LIST FOR OFFICE FURNITURE

_____ desk

_____ desk chair

_____ wastebasket

_____ file cabinet(s)

_____ extra desk chair(s)

_____ in and out baskets

_____ bookshelves and other storage

_____ coffeepot or teapot and cups

_____ dishes, kitchen supplies

_____ clock

_____ bulletin board

_____ sofa or armchair

_____ table

_____ radio and/or television

_____ fan and/or air conditioner

_____ lamps

_____ art to hang on walls

_____ pencil and pen holder

OTHER OFFICE SERVICES

Another element of setting up an office involves arranging for support services such as copying and printing, messengers, cleaning, and possibly coffee and other vending services. Make sure these suppliers are easily accessible to you and shop around to find the best sources in terms of price and quality of service.

Although hiring a cleaning service may sound extravagant, especially if you work at home, it is fully tax deductible, relatively inexpensive, and takes care of a task most freelancers, who already spend long hours at work, do not want to bother with.

BUYING OFFICE SUPPLIES

"I knew I was becoming a real businesswoman when I started avidly reading the office supply catalogs that arrived in my mail," says one new entrepreneur. "I soon discovered that another freelancer I knew was developing a similar affection for office supplies, and the next thing I knew, one of us would jokingly call the other whenever she had made a 'major' purchase or found some new item for the office. It was all a joke, but it was also a lot of fun."

Freelancers do indeed find that treating themselves to office supplies can be fun, and why not? They are tax deductible, and as the freelancer who just described her burgeoning love of office supplies notes, "On a bad day, it's a lot cheaper than hitting Saks Fifth Avenue." The amounts and kinds of office supplies you need vary with the nature of your business, but the following list will set you up with the basics:

_____ pens

_____ pencils

_____ erasers

_____ computer, copy, and fax paper

_____ notepads in assorted sizes

_____ paper clips

_____ rubber bands

_____ stapler and staples

_____ scissors

_____ tape (clear tape and mailing tape) and tape dispenser

_____ brown paper for wrapping packages

_____ stamps

_____ envelopes in several sizes

_____ mailing labels

_____ clipboard

_____ Rolodex or other storage file for names, addresses, and phone numbers

_____ filing supplies

Business Cards and Stationery

In addition to basic office supplies, you need to buy stationery and business cards. These two items are especially important because, like advertising, they help to shape your image. Fortunately today it is possible to buy high-quality stationery and cards without spending a lot of money. Some freelancers even use desktop publishing programs to create their own letterheads and business cards.

Stationery and cards come in all levels of quality and prices, ranging from instant printing to engraved printing. Unless you can afford to do so, there is no reason to get very fancy, and in some businesses you can even skip a card. A good rule of thumb is that you need a card if you are frequently asked for one; if no one ever asks to see your card, then you don't need one. One freelancer who moved her editing services business from Minneapolis to Chicago notes, "I had cards printed when I started in Minneapolis. Then when I moved I was on a tight budget and never got around to having new cards made. I discovered that even though people occasionally asked me for my card, no one was upset when I said I didn't have one. I've never gotten new cards." On the subject of cards and stationery, simple is better than fancy. One freelance typesetter says, "I got very carried away with my cards when I started out. After all, letters were my business. I made myself an oversized and beautiful card. Then gradually, as I became friends with the people I worked for, one or two admitted that they found my cards inconvenient because they were too large to fit into a Rolodex. I tossed out my lovely cards and got myself a plainer, standard-sized card."

The cheapest and most practical way to obtain stationery is to print it yourself, using a computer and a good desktop printing software program. With these tools, you can design an array of paper products for less than they would cost if produced by someone else. You do need a very good printer, probably laser, to produce stationery that truly rivals what a professional printer will do.

If you opt for this method of creating stationery and business cards, do try to approximate what you would buy if you purchased these products. The temptation is to do something very creative, even eccentric, simply because you have the means to do so. But it is probably better to put these creative urges to work on your personal writing papers rather than on your business stationery, especially when you are just starting out.

The next cheapest way to obtaining stationery is to let an instant printer use his or her software program and computer to produce it for you. Depending on the design you select, instant printers charge from $15 to $50 for several hundred business cards. One hundred sheets of imprinted stationery and envelopes will cost anywhere from $30 to $150 from an instant printer. They would cost several hundred dollars more if you had them engraved.

Whatever method you use, the first step is to choose a typeface, which you will do in conjunction with the printer, who can offer advice. Type comes in many different styles, called typefaces, and sizes. Type for a letterhead, usually a one-time expense since you can reuse it when you reprint, costs from $20 to $200, depending on the kind you select.

Once the type is set, you should insist on proofing it. Even if the proof consists only of your name, address, telephone and fax numbers, there is room for error, and it is better to catch it now than when the job is finished. It helps to supply the typesetter with clean, clearly typed copy.

The next step is to choose a paper. As a general rule, go for something conservative, unless you are in a very creative business where something brightly colored or extravagantly designed is called for. The instant printer will have a line of papers or possibly several lines from which to choose, and you can also supply your own paper. Art supply stores carry a variety of papers for this purpose. Buy at least a 20 weight so the paper does not appear flimsy. White, gray, buff, tan, and ivory are the most acceptable business paper colors. You can never go wrong with one of these shades.

Instant printers also usually offer a line of noncustom stationery. You peruse a sample book with many kinds of letterheads and choose the one you like. This may suit your needs very well and may be less expensive.

Attractive stationery and business cards can also be ordered from direct-mail suppliers. The best, such as Merrimade (1-800-344-4256), offer a very good selection of high-quality papers at reasonable cost. Labels and other paper goods can also be ordered from mail-order services.

The most expensive and handsome kind of stationery you can buy is engraved. This is an old-fashioned method of printing, and elegant and attractive as it is, engraving is usually beyond the means of most freelancers, at least initially. But it is perhaps something you will treat yourself to when you are successful.

An engraver makes a plate with the type you need on it. This plate is then used to print the paper. The plate, whose creation involves a separate and fairly hefty cost, can be reused. Some mail-order house offer both printing and engraving. Major jewelers, such as Tiffany and Cartier, also do engraving.

Most freelancers opt for stationery without a logo, probably because they do not want to go to the expense of having one designed. If you do decide on a logo—perhaps you can select a stock one offered by your printer—keep it simple. One successful copy editor–typist has a small typewriter on her letterhead. It is simple, it gets her point across, and makes her correspondence—especially invoices—stand out on someone's desk. It is a logo that works. Fancy type and overdesigned logos often do not work, and they make your letterhead difficult to read.

Once you get your stationery, be careful how you use it, strange as this may sound. Certainly you should type invoices on it, as well as confirming letters and letters of agreement. But resist the urge to write a letter when a phone call will do the job. Editor Chuck Wall explained why he views letterheads and fancy cards with some degree of suspicion: "When I see the letterhead, I often think this is someone who is going to nag me. I like to speak to freelancers face-to-face. People who have letterheads tend to be the people who write you every month and who send you Christmas cards and postcards when they go away on vacation. You dread hearing from them because they nag you by letter during the months when you don't have work. You get letterhead after letterhead from them." The message from

Wall and several other people who hire freelancers is that letterheads are great for invoicing and legitimate business communications. But where the custom of more direct encounters, either in person or by telephone, exists, as it does in publishing and many other areas where freelancers work, you should follow that custom. You will only appear unnecessarily stiff and formal if you use your letterhead where you could better use a telephone.

Shopping for Office Supplies

Before signing off on the subject of office supplies, here are a few pointers on buying and using them:

- Whenever possible, buy in bulk. Many office supply stores offer a 10 to 15 percent discount for quantity purchases. Often, items are not displayed in bulk, but don't let this stop you. Ask for a box of typewriter ribbons or a box of pens or whatever you need.
- But don't buy too much. While buying in bulk is fun and feels businesslike, it has its downside. Office supplies are bulky and hard to store, and besides, if you buy tons of computer paper, you will not feel like buying it when it is on sale.
- Think about buying recycled paper. You may not want your stationery and business card printed on recycled paper, which still tends to be a little gray, but recycled computer paper satisfactory for most uses is now available. As of this writing, you will still pay a premium of about 10 percent for recycled paper.
- Shop by direct mail. A number of excellent mail-order catalogs cater to small businesses, supplying everything from discounted printer ribbons to paper supplies to office furniture. One excellent direct-mail outlet is Lyben Computer Systems (1-800-493-5777). They offer a big selection of all kinds of office supplies (their name is misleading), keep their prices down, and ship within twenty-four hours. Offering great quality and style at a very fair price is a stationery specialist called Merri-made (1-800-344-4256). These are just two of many direct mail catalogs.

- Shop discount. Major office-supply discounters—Staples is one of the biggest, best, and most available—now have stores in malls and other shopping districts of most cities.

  Office discounters often sell only in bulk. This can be good or bad, depending upon your needs. Do not be forced into buying more than you need in order to get a discount. Discounters also sell very basic goods. So if you are looking for anything at all unusual (index cards or file folders in five colors, for example), you still may do better with direct mail.

- Buy stamps in bulk because it saves time. You go to the post office less often. Stamps are sold in rolls of a hundred, and for a ridiculously low price of about 5 cents, you can buy a plain plastic container for a roll of stamps. In a stationery store, decorative containers cost $5 to $10.

- Reuse office supplies as much as possible. Envelopes can easily be reused; files can be used over and over. One freelancer admits: "I'm a shameless reuser of envelopes, and I don't care if I send one client something in an envelope from another client. I figure it's a not-too-subtle way to let one know I have other business. On the other hand, if I'm just starting to work with someone, I usually want to impress him or her with my neatness and sense of organization, so I make an effort to send materials in a fresh envelope—the first couple of times, anyway."

- If you travel a lot for business, or call on clients, set up a briefcase desk so you aren't always dashing around at the last minute before an appointment looking for the office supplies you need. Stock your briefcase or tote bag with invoices, cards, notepads, pencils and pens, envelopes, stamps, and anything else you need.

- If something saves you time, consider buying it. Time is very valuable to freelancers, and something that might look like a luxury can actually be a good time-saver. For example, one freelance editor bought preprinted labels, which came only in a quantity of 500 and cost considerably more than the plain ones she could buy in a stationery store. She thought she was doing this because she hated addressing envelopes, and she joked with friends about having to order 500—a quantity that seemed impossible to use up even over a period of several years. To her surprise, the labels turned out to be real time-savers, and she uses them at the rate of about 150 a year. The initial investment of $30 now seems cheap. Remember that one freelancer's time- and money-saver might be another's luxury. These decisions are personal, but once you realize that something saves *you* money, make sure you stock it.

OFFICE "ACCESSORIES"

More than other small business owners, freelancers tend to carry their work with them. Since we are home-based, we call on clients rather than the other way around, and this means we need especially appealing and businesslike briefcases, portfolios, and dare I even say it, totes. While these items are not, strictly speaking, office equipment, this may be the time to discuss them since anyone who is setting up an office is also probably thinking about these vital accessories.

These are image builders, and for this reason alone it is important to buy the best quality you can afford. Leather is nice, but a well-designed canvas briefcase also can work well, as can nylon and other synthetics, provided they do not look cheap.

Ironically, although you should buy something nice, there is such a thing as too nice. Unless you are in the fashion business, a $1,000 designer briefcase or tote can be off-putting, suggesting perhaps that you do not exactly need to work for a living. A classy, well-designed briefcase or portfolio, on the other hand, has a job to do, and that is to announce that you are worth the price you will be charging.

OFFICE SECURITY

The final thing you have to worry about as you set up an office is how to protect it. Burglary or fire in your workplace can be even more devastating than a burglary or fire in your home. You can lose work-in-progress, your file of business contacts and financial records, as well as samples of work.

Taking Inventory

Once your office is settled, you should make an inventory so you have proof of what you own. An inventory will also help you and your insurance agent decide what kind and how much insurance you need. Your homeowner's or business policy may not cover such things as blank checks, manuscripts, and certain records—the very things that you may consider most important. To make a simple office inventory:

1. List each item, the year it was purchased, its original cost, and its present value.
2. List the model number, brand name, dealer's name, and a description of the item. Save and attach receipts.
3. If you have unique, expensive items—a Tiffany desk lamp or a Biedermeier desk, for example,—a Polaroid snapshot is a good idea.
4. Keep a copy of this inventory in a safe place other than your office (a safe deposit box, for example).
5. Update the inventory regularly, possibly as often as every three or six months while you are still buying major items for your office. At minimum, update it once a year.

Physical Protection

A minimum level of protection involves buying a good lock for the door and locks for the windows. Beyond that, consider either a burglar alarm or a safe—or possibly both. Safes are designed for specific tasks, that is, they are either burglarproof or they are fireproof, so you have to decide which is more important to you. You can, of course, purchase a safe that is both, but it will cost you approximately $1,200, a figure that is out of reach for most freelancers. A good fireproof safe, fifteen by eighteen by twelve inches in size, costs about $400–$500;

a similar-size safe that is burglarproof costs about $500. Before you buy either one, check with your insurance agent to see if there are any specific requirements that you can afford to meet. Locksmiths often point out that insurance companies have rather unreasonable requirements regarding safes that few small business operators actually can afford to meet, but you should check just the same.

Buy the best safe you can afford. Bolt it to something in the office; very large safes have been carried away by enterprising burglars. Never leave the combination anywhere in the office. Even if you have a safe, never leave checks, credit cards, or cash in it.

A burglar alarm offers a second form of security to an office. Best of all is one that rings in a protection agency or a police station, if you live in a community small enough so that police intercept these calls. Such systems are expensive, however, and you may be able to afford only a local alarm that makes enough noise to scare off a prospective burglar. On-site alarms work best when attached to safes or lock boxes. Before purchasing a burglar system, talk to several professionals to get their estimates of what you need and what it should cost.

Organizing and setting up an office is something most freelancers approach with a great deal of enthusiasm. Unlike an office that belongs to your employer, your own office—whether it is in your home or outside your home—bears your personal stamp. It can and should be organized exactly to your taste and needs, and this is surely one of the better "perks" of freelancing.

5

NEW OFFICE TECHNOLOGY

TECHNOLOGY HAS DRAMATICALLY AND PERMANENTLY transformed the world of business. And as important as this transformation is to big business, it is even more so to small businesses—and by extension to freelancers. It has streamlined many of the functions and operations of business, which in turn saves precious time and enables businesses to compete more effectively. Without using some aspect of the new technology, it is doubtful that a freelancer can remain competitive.

Given this, it is amazing to learn that only 40 percent of small businesses own computers. And of those that do, a sizable number have not plugged them in. In countless offices and homes around the country, desktop computers sit in an out-of-the-way corner, untouched, gathering dust, which by the way is a natural enemy of the computer.

What accounts for this stunning display of Luddism? Only one thing: cyberphobia, or fear of computers, a condition that seems to strike freelancers in numbers that are disproportionately large compared to other small-business owners. Perhaps because we are such small operations, we fear, with some justification, that we will lose records that will then require hours of our time to duplicate. We worry that we will lose valuable time whenever our computer is down. And we stew that we will have to learn a new skill—another time-consuming activity that will drain off hours from our "real" work.

Yet computers are invaluable to any freelance operation. They offer a speedier, more accurate way to budget and watch cash flow. They help identify customers' needs. They track inventory. They help to collect accounts receivable. In many fields such as publishing, design, television, and film, the very nature of creative work has been redefined.

While it is true that computers were initially expensive and at times tricky to learn to use, even unreliable, this is no longer the case. Prices have dropped dramatically, software has improved 1,000 percent, and reliability is no longer an excuse any freelancer can use for not computerizing.

The new technology is quite simply something you cannot afford to live without. What is still a minefield for the cautious or inexperienced freelancers is how you go about choosing and shopping for technology. Without mentioning brand names or giving you guidelines that will be dated before this book is published, this chapter will walk you through the new technology and show you how to put it to work for you.

ADVANTAGES AND DISADVANTAGES

The thing technology does best is give you access to better and more information. You can get it faster, and it is more timely and accurate. The new technology, especially computers, makes your work more interesting. No longer do you have to spend hours every day or week monitoring inventory or doing bookkeeping. Business operations—mostly monotonous ones—that used to consume hours now can be performed literally in minutes, if not seconds.

With all these advantages, there are still some disadvantages. The first and perhaps biggest is expense. All technology is expensive when it is new, and although prices come down rapidly after a new product is introduced, equipment still represents a considerable investment for a freelancer. Business equipment must often be more up-to-date and powerful than home equipment.

A good business computer costs $2,500 to $3,500. A computer-aided design (CAD) software program geared to a specific business starts at about $7,000. A solid telecommunications system costs hundreds of dollars. Photocopiers can be purchased for as little as $200, but most freelancers find themselves needing one that costs $800 to $1,200.

The second disadvantage is obsolescence. New technology does not stay new very long. Every few years, completely new stuff comes along to replace the "old" stuff. It usually does not pay to hang on to the old, and smart freelancers plan not only their present but also their future purchases once they open the door to technology.

Mistakes can be costly. If you buy the wrong equipment, you have bought a white elephant, and you may not be able to do much about it except start saving for the right equipment. If the wrong information is entered or it is incorrectly entered into a computer, to cite another common problem, hours, days, weeks, even months may be required to remedy the situation.

Technology, especially computers, causes anxiety. It can make people feel inept and outdated. They worry whether they can learn how to use new equipment. The short answer to this question is yes, you absolutely can. My seventy-eight-year-old mother has learned how to use a computer.

One real problem is that some freelancers tend to rely too much on technology and in the process fail to trust their intuition as much as they should. A wealth of data involving your customers, for example, can be at your fingertips with a computer, but this is no substitute for what your gut instinct tells you is right—or wrong—about your customers' needs.

A graphic designer installed a state-of-the-art telecommunications system. It not only answered his phone but it announced callers orally and then directed them either to voice mail or to one of three informational messages about his services. So enamored did the designer become with this system that he rarely answered his phone, and he never returned calls before the end of the work day. Only when several clients told him point-blank they could no longer work with him because he was so inaccessible did he rethink his use of technology.

An author discovered that her writing was suffering from too much technology. At her computer, she tended to spend her time fiddling with the small details and not fixing the big picture. Only when she decided to sit down and completely reenter her manuscript—as she would have had to do with a typewriter—was she able to polish her work in the way it demanded. Computers can and should do a lot for you, but they are not a substitute for occasionally picking up a pad and paper and brainstorming the old-fashioned way.

Despite the disadvantages, there is no denying that adding a computer—the most important of the new technologies—to your office or studio opens endless possibilities for enhancing your work. A freelance ceramics restorer used her computer to locate new clients. After spending only a few hours browsing the Web, she discovered a list of small museums around the country that might need her services. She used desktop publishing to create a brochure, which she both snail-mailed and E-mailed to the prospective clients she had found.

Her efforts netted her six solid prospects, one of which was a small southwestern museum featuring Native American pottery. When the curator became nervous about the fact that her studio was 4,000 miles from his museum, she was able to show him—via E-mail— exactly how she intended to re-create lost designs on pottery. She got the job and eventually became a specialist in restoring Native American pottery.

HOW TO BUY TECHNOLOGY

Because big business spends millions of dollars on technology, it needs to evaluate each purchase carefully before buying. On a much smaller scale, freelancers can do the same thing. Here are six steps that will guide any business through the process of selecting and buying technology.

1. Assess your needs. Do you need a sophisticated telecommunications system, or will a simple answering system and a two-line telephone do the job for you? How will you use a desktop computer? Will it perform accounting functions, or will you use it to provide your service? Will you use it for on-line research? Rank your uses and needs in order of importance.

2. Decide how much you can afford. What is important enough that you must purchase it now? What can wait? If you decide you need an $8,000 CAD software system, you may not be able to afford a photocopier. Setting a budget and sticking to it will enable to you to spread out your technology purchases in a way that is efficient and kind to your pocketbook.

3. Identify the technology that serves your needs. Technology changes rapidly, so for this you will need to rely on salespeople and experts. Read magazines and newspapers to see what's new, especially specialized ones such as *Home Office Computing*, which caters to small and home offices. Computer magazines constantly rate new products.

   If possible, weigh not only your present needs but future ones as well. If you need a photocopier, but your research shows that a new generation of copiers due out next year will be a major leap forward in speed and efficiency, then it may make sense to wait. You will spend more (and have more time to save), but you will also benefit by having a machine that you can use for a long time, far longer than if you bought a machine that was on the verge of obsolescence. On the other hand, if your photocopying needs are fairly straightforward, maybe you can take advantage of rock-bottom prices and buy the old model now while it is at the end of its production run.

4. Shop. You have several options here. Major discounters have begun competing with smaller specialized stores and department stores. In addition, new equipment can be purchased by mail order. One major computer manufacturer, Dell, sells by mail.

   Another decision is whether to buy a known brand or a lesser-known one. A few years ago, American consumers were entirely oriented toward brand names, but this is no longer true. Many excellent lesser-known manufacturers deliver a good product—and better savings.

5. Install the technology. Computers require extensive setting up. The operating system must be installed, along with all the software you have purchased. Especially for the technology-illiterate-and-proud-of-it set, this requires only that you hire a computer nerd, that specialized breed of expert who knows how to hook up anything transistorized.

   Incidentally, this is one time not to overlook child labor. Lots of college and even high school kids understand this stuff inside and out and can do an efficient, effective job of setting up your equipment. Obviously, if you buy a certain kind of equipment, for example, a photocopier or a telephone system, you should expect service from the manufacturer. This is something to find out when you purchase the equipment.

6. Use it. This especially applies to computers. The biggest and most expensive mistake a freelancer can make is to buy equipment and then not use it. If you do not understand, or cannot teach yourself, how to use the technology you have purchased, then hire someone to tutor you. Most people, however, are perfectly capable of teaching themselves to use a computer. The learning curve is steep initially, but it levels off rather quickly. Just when you think you will never master it, suddenly everything becomes much clearer. After this most people learn quickly.

Two Rules You Cannot Ignore

The first rule is to buy all the technology you can possibly afford. It doesn't pay to buy less than you need with the idea of upgrading gradually. Technology does not work that way. It moves far too fast for this strategy to be efficient.

The second rule is to expect obsolescence in five years. Even sooner if you don't pay attention to the first rule. Fortunately, this is the length of time the IRS allows to depreciate equipment. (Technology manufacturers must *know* this.)

Now let's talk about what's available and what's useful to freelancers.

DESKTOP COMPUTER

Of all the new technologies, the most important and necessary is the desktop computer. Because they are expensive and multifaceted, they arc also sometimes the scariest piece of equipment to buy—all the more reason to put yourself through the aforementioned paces before taking the plunge.

More than with any other piece of equipment, it is important to buy enough computer. As of this writing, for an IBM-compatible, this would mean at least 8 to 16 megabytes of RAM, a 1- to 2-gigabite hard drive, a high-density floppy disk drive, CD-ROM, a mouse, a color monitor, a Pentium processor, and a modem. (A modem is necessary to use E-mail, belong to an on-line service such as Compuserve or America Online, and browse the Web. You also need specialized software.)

Unknown brands can be good purchases provided the product comes highly recommended by computer gurus. All desktop computers, though, emulate either IBM or Apple, the two companies that have brought us two somewhat different operating systems. Basically the difference is between using an icon-oriented machine versus a character-based one. Apple is icon-oriented. This means you employ a mouse to point to a picture of a wastebasket when you do not want to save your work, or you point to a picture of a file when you do want to save it. In contrast, IBM and IBM clones use characters, that is, when you store a file, you press the F2 key, or when you want to exit, you press F7.

Character-oriented manufacturers have tried to become more icon-oriented through the use of software like Windows, but these efforts have not been entirely successful. And there is a downside to

Apple's icons. Far more software has been created for IBM and its clones because there are far more IBM clones in the world than there are Apples and its clones. (Partly this is because Apple did not permit cloning until very recently.)

A good computer costs between $2,000 and $3,000.

Hardware and Software

A computer, plus the printer and any other accessories, is called the hardware. The programs you must buy in order to make the computer operate are called software.

Software programs are designed for both general and specialized use. General programs create computer-generated design, do word processing, or prepare spreadsheets, while specialized softwares are programs that do only accounting or only communications. Even more specialized programs might perform accounting for freelance editors or design for architects.

When buying software it is also often possible to choose integrated software—that is, software that performs all the major functions you need. At minimum, most freelancers will need some kind of accounting and a word-processing software. A computer specialist can help you pinpoint your needs even more. If you have a need, chances are the software has been created to meet it. There are specialized programs for almost every field and every business function.

Software varies greatly in price. A very simple, one-function program sometimes can be purchased for as little as $40, while you will spend around $400 for a good word-processing or spreadsheet program and several thousand dollars on a specialized design program. General-use software programs, including the operating software, are typically bundled with the price of a computer. This is often the least expensive way to buy them.

LAPTOP COMPUTER

A laptop makes a good backup computer, and you can travel with it. It is even possible to satisfy all your needs with a laptop, since these now pack as much power—and sometimes more—as desktops. A laptop suitable for business use costs at least $2,000.

FAX MACHINE

After computers, fax machines have done the most to revolutionize life for freelancers. Nobody seems to want to use snail (or regular) mail anymore, not when something can arrive instantly via fax. A fax machine uses the telephone wires to transmit a facsimile of whatever is sent. Put a letter in a fax machine, and your client has it in his or her hands within seconds. Fax machines also function as single-sheet photocopiers. They can be purchased for under $400.

SCANNER

This high-tech computer accessory scans material into a computer. You can now buy a scanner that is built in to your keyboard, your computer, your fax machine, or your telephone.

Depending on the level of sophistication you need, a scanner will cost you anywhere from $300 to $1,500.

PHOTOCOPIER

This popular machine, which is now available in home-use sizes, saves you trips and money spent at the local copy store. The small-format machines are expensive to operate, though, so make sure you really need one before you go shopping. These can also be high-maintenance machines.

The trick is to buy enough machine to really serve your purposes. A slow copier may drive you crazy and send you running to the local copy store, and yet another machine gathers dust in your office.

Photocopiers vary in price from $400 to several thousand dollars.

TELECOMMUNICATIONS SYSTEM

Your telecommunications system is crucial. Don't forget that when you worked for someone, you were provided with a receptionist, voice mail, an order department, and so on—all things you must now provide for your customers.

Telecommunications systems have become very sophisticated in the past few years. In the not-too-distant future it will be routine to buy a telecommunications system that is built into a computer. A variety of services that aid freelancers are available now, such as call forwarding, call answering, call waiting, caller ID, and voice mail. One of the more helpful services is call organizer. For a small monthly fee, your phone bill can specify which calls are to be billed to which clients.

Caller ID makes a great deal of sense for the harried freelancer. You can screen your calls and route certain ones to either voice mail or any of several prerecorded messages.

Telecommunications systems vary enormously depending on what you buy. A phone machine can be purchased for under $100, while a sophisticated multiline system can cost thousands.

CELLULAR TELEPHONE

Cellular telephones are proving valuable for some freelancers. One television producer who purchased one saw his business increase in one year by 50 percent. Discreet inquiries to his clients, both new and old, revealed that the only improvement was the fact that he was so much more accessible by telephone.

When you buy a cellular phone, you purchase only the phone. You still need a service contract to use it. You should treat your server the same as your long-distance company and shop around periodically to be sure you are getting the best deal. Like the regular phone companies, cellular phone servers offer a wide range of usage plans. For example, some cellular suppliers have an option that bills the calling party for any calls they make. Your customers will not be happy with this. Your friends will not be happy, either, but at least with them, you are more likely to get a chance to explain. This will definitely be a factor in the server you choose.

Finally, remember that what looks cheap may not be. A cellular phone package that costs $30 a month with free calls for the first thirty minutes is no bargain if every call over thirty minutes costs 50 cents, and you spend hours on the cell phone every month.

Cell phone prices vary greatly depending on where you live and the kind of package you arrange. As of this writing, cellular phone packages cost about $30 a month. Two years ago, the average package hovered between $50 to $80 a month, so prices are headed downward.

BEEPERS

Beepers, like cell phones, are enormously useful to the freelancer who is away from the phone during working hours. Beepers cost $10 to $25 per month; the service provides the beeper.

A SHOPPING GUIDE

With such varying price ranges, it is obviously important to shop wisely for any office technology. Here are some hints on doing this:

- Comparison shop. And don't just look at one kind of vendor. Weigh the department store price against a mail-order price. Find out about lesser-known brands.
- Look into buyer services. Many professional organizations offer these as a benefit, and they also exist on-line, or you can sometimes join one independently.
- Consider the hidden costs. A photocopier that is $400 may have a per-page cost of 12 cents, whereas one that costs $1,000 may have a per-page costs of 2 cents. Which is cheapest in the long run? Similarly, the cost of operating a laser printer ranges from 18 to 25 cents per page, after factoring in toner and paper.

Most technology has a cost beyond the initial price of the machine. Some require regular maintenance; others are expensive to maintain or to use. A photocopier runs about $800 a year to use; a fax machine, about $350; a cellular phone service contract costs about $430 annually.

- Ask friends and associates about their experiences. This is often the best way to find out what is right for you. Ask strangers, too. Sending a query for advice out to on-line friends is another good way to gather consumer information.

- Consider leasing. It can be cheaper than buying. With some equipment, it is worthwhile because of the service that comes with a lease. If you need a photocopier and will give it heavy use, you may be better off leasing rather than buying. Virtually any piece of office equipment you can think of can be leased. Another advantage to leasing is that you can take a tax deduction on the machine forever, whereas equipment you purchase is typically depreciated over five years.

SPACE-SAVING TIPS

After you buy the equipment, you have to have someplace to put it. Machines may make you more efficient, but too many machines in too small a space can make you inefficient. You will not use a scanner if you have to take it out of a closet each time you need it, nor will you use a photocopier whose surface is covered with books and papers.

Two solutions, used in tandem, are required to keep the high-tech office organized. The first is to plan a place for your new purchases before you buy them. If necessary, hire the services of an office decorator or a professional organizer. The second solution is to look for space-saving equipment. Here are some hints on doing this:

- Buy a tower CPU for your computer. Having a vertical instead of a horizontal unit saves space.
- Save space with a laptop instead of a desktop computer.

- Think about using cellular and cordless phones. Phone wires are a major problem in many offices, and they are unsightly.
- Go multimedia. The technology is there. You have only to decide to spend the money on it. Buy a computer with internal speakers. Let your CD-ROM function as your in-office disk player. Buy a scanner keyboard or a computer with a built-in telephone.

HEALTH CONCERNS

A number of people avoid computers and other technology because of health concerns. While much of what has been written about the dangers of computers and other high-technology equipment is not proved, health is a concern, although the main hazard is the toll that long hours at a computer can take on your physical wellbeing. Technology presents some hazards, but not so much that we should avoid using it.

Research has shown, for example, that video display terminals do not emit dangerous levels of either ultraviolet rays or ionizing radiation. As a result, protective screens are not necessary. When working at a monitor, though, you should do what you can to prevent eyestrain, dryness, and irritation, as well as the temporary myopia that troubles some people who spend long hours in front of a computer. Here are some hints on protecting your eyes while you work at a computer:

- Eliminate glare on the computer screen. Position the monitor at a right angle to windows or lights rather than in front or in back of them. Slightly tinted lenses are helpful if you wear glasses, as are computer hoods or micromesh filters that can be attached to the monitor.
- Don't work in an overly dark room.
- Do put light on your reading material, which should be placed to the right or left of you or alongside the monitor.
- Take frequent breaks during the day. Try to look away from the

screen (and your work!) at least every fifteen minutes. Stand up and stretch at least once an hour, more often if possible. Walk away from your desk. Move your arms around. Very gently move your head from right to left. Shrug your shoulders a few times. In other words, move the body parts that stay most rigid while you are working at the computer.

- Get routine eye exams if you are a regular computer user, especially if you are experiencing temporary myopia, a condition in which distant objects appear a little blurry for a few minutes after you look up from the monitor.
- If you wear glasses or contacts, be sure your ophthalmologist knows you work at a computer screen. Perhaps your prescription can be adjusted to help you. People who have graduated to bifocals often find it helpful to have a pair of glasses they wear only at the computer.

Carpel Tunnel Syndrome

The other major health problem associated with computer use is carpel tunnel syndrome, wrist pain that results from the repetitive movements at a keyboard. To avoid this, many of the same suggestions that work for eyes can be applied to the rest of your body. Do not sit rigidly at a computer for hours, but instead, take frequent breaks to move your body around.

Keep your wrists straight as you work. Do not hold them in a flexed, extended, or twisted position. Some people find that a pad under their wrists helps, although recent research suggests that this may not put your wrists in the best position either. Another measure that helps some people is the split keyboard.

Health Concerns and Photocopiers

Photocopiers emit some ozone. However appropriate this gas is for the outer layer of air on our planet, it is an irritant when it is in the air we breathe. But with proper ventilation and maintenance, no photocopier should emit harmful levels of this substance.

Toner dust is another irritant, especially to the eyes. If you see toner dust, it is a good idea to turn off the photocopier until you can get it serviced.

THE ERGONOMIC OFFICE

Anyone who works with a computer has a special reason to design an office that is as ergonomic as possible. This is one of the most important things you can do to eliminate the general physical strain, the neck or head or backaches that are too often the toll of working all day at a computer.

Unfortunately, the kind of physical strain that comes from hunching over an ill-fitting desk for long hours is usually cumulative. It may not hurt at first to work at a desk that is ergonomically incorrect or otherwise improperly arranged, but after years of doing so you will find that what was once an occasional ache or pain has become a full-blown chronic pain.

It is far better to prevent the pain than to deal with it after the fact. To this end, experts have devised what they believe to be an ergonomically correct desk. They have worked out how many inches your head should be from your monitor, the distance between your eyes and the keyboard, the correct height of your desk, and most important, if only because it is so often ignored, the correct angle for viewing the screen. The following drawing gives the average proportions that will help you work comfortably.

Keep in mind that these measurements are only averages. If you are very short or very tall, you may have to make adjustments. I once bought a computer desk, for example, that was an ergonomically correct 28 inches from the floor. To my dismay, it was very painful to work at it. I thought I had suddenly developed the world's worst case of carpel tunnel syndrome. Only when I took my keyboard down another inch and bought a footrest did my workplace become comfortable again. So experiment to find what works best for you. If necessary, hire an ergonomics expert to study your office and adjust it to you specifically.

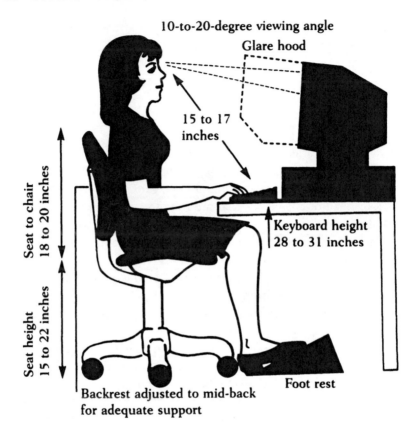

While it may seem odd to end a chapter on technology on a note of comfort, it is also perhaps ironically appropriate. In order to use technology well, you need to be comfortable with it—both physically and mentally. The purpose of this chapter has been to bring you to that point, to enable you see how technology can help you do your work better, more efficiently, and more profitably.

6

THE FINANCES OF
FREELANCING

FREELANCERS MAY BE AFRAID OF THE TAX man, but they are down-right apathetic about planning their financial lives. This may in fact be a major factor in the high attrition rate for freelancers. It certainly is what separates the business-oriented—and financially success-ful—freelancers from the independent spirits who are often too poor to enjoy their independence. The most common failing is not keep-ing a good set of records. Without that, a freelancer has difficulty measuring success in financial terms as well as planning for the fu-ture.

Research done by the Small Business Administration indicates that poor record keeping is a major reason for the high rate of business failures for small businesses. A good record-keeping system increases your chances of staying in business and earning large profits.

For the majority of freelancers, though, record keeping is some-thing of a short suit, one that most are not even particularly inter-ested in, as this statement by an advertising copywriter shows: "Today, I'm pretty decent about the whole thing. I do try to stay tuned to these matters. But when I started out, I was rotten. The only thing I did was pay the IRS. Were I to start all over today, I would structure my business differently. I would begin with an accountant who specializes in freelancers. I would have him set up a records system I could easily follow—and one that didn't take too much time." A weaver concurs: "I know I should have a separate business account. I should at least have a retirement account—that is something I could do for me. But I resist the whole notion of getting involved with that stuff. I freelance because I like the feeling of freedom, and I guess I'm afraid I won't feel so free if I have to spend several hours a week filling in record books."

Unfortunately, small-business owners tend to receive more formal help than freelancers do. If you have a bank loan, you are likely to have a banker looking over your shoulder, or at a minimum you were forced to do some financial planning, which was, in turn, reviewed by a bank officer. The Small Business Administration is more geared to small businesses than to freelancers. Small-business centers at colleges and universities often focus on small businesses to the exclusion of freelancers.

We freelancers generally have to rely on our wits. Fortunately, many of us, even the creative types, discover the hidden pleasures of financial housekeeping. Some, such as furniture designer-painter Connie Pfander, are delighted to discover that they're really quite adept at managing their finances. Pfander reports, "I always thought I couldn't add two and two and stayed away from numbers. But then, when I was thinking about setting up my freelance business, I took another freelance job as office manager for some SoHo clothes designers. They called in their accountant and had him show me how to keep the books. I thought I was going to hate that, but to my surprise I really loved it. I did those books very diligently, and in the process I learned a lot that eventually helped me get a loan to finance my own freelance business." She adds, "I know lots of artists and craftspeople who think they shouldn't be bothered with paperwork because they are creative people. But since I've gotten involved in furniture design, I also have met lots of craftspeople who are very good at the financial end of their businesses. I now think that creativity and good financial sense can go hand in hand. At least, there's no truth to the image of scatterbrained and disorganized artists. It just doesn't have to be that way."

Another good planner is rights and permissions editor Barbara Zimmerman, who says, "I kept good records right from the beginning because I comprehended immediately that my expenses came off my income taxes, and that I had to keep track of them. I keep daily copies of my expenses. I debit instantly which expenses belong to which client. I keep a minimal sort of books, though.

"My financial planning is, unfortunately, even more minimal, although I'm very interested in learning more about that. I used to hold off all December money and didn't deposit it when it came in the mail. I am finally starting to learn about insurance policies and money. I have a retirement plan, and I'm trying to figure out how to earn more money on that. My business account is separate from my personal account."

Most freelancers are neither so antibookkeeping as the weaver nor so astute as the furniture designer. Most keep few or no accurate records; many do not even know how to go about setting up a records system.

SETTING UP A RECORD-KEEPING SYSTEM

All freelancers need to do two things to organize their financial lives. The first is to set up and maintain a record-keeping system to record the daily, weekly, and monthly flow of cash through the business. The second is to create a budget and a cash-flow chart that can be used to analyze present and future cash flow to see how you are doing. Both activities help to track the money that flows through the business. Without an awareness of how much money you have received and spent, as well as how much you anticipate receiving and spending in the future, it is impossible to know how the business is doing.

A record-keeping system can be simple or complicated, but it need not be the latter to be effective and useful. You can have your accountant set up a record-keeping system, but you should work with it yourself, at least for the first few years you are in business. No one else will ever care as much about the money your business earns as you do, so it is important for you to have a complete grasp of the finances of your business before turning the reins over to someone else.

Even if you hire a bookkeeper or an accountant, it is important that you understand what he or she is doing with your money.

Your financial records are an important part of your business. You need orderly records to obtain a bank loan. You also need them for insurance claims and for any litigation involving money. Finally, they are IRS records. Although the IRS has never specified what records business owners should maintain, you need your financial records to justify the deductions you take on your taxes and to show how much money your business has earned. Many accountants, in fact, advise business owners never to throw away the financial records relating to an existing business.

Every records system should be easy to use, up-to-date, and accurate. Fortunately, a freelancer's records system can be highly personal, even idiosyncratic. One freelance author keeps her financial records in several three-ring notebooks. One contains invoices, contracts, letters of agreements, royalty statements, budgets, and other records regarding payments. She records expenses in a notebook she carries with her. Another notebook contains all the business correspondence she writes during the course of one year that is related to her finances. This system works well for her since she often has to put her hands on certain pieces of information quickly while she is on the phone. She comments: "I ghostwrite for a woman, so we share royalties. Often when we're discussing business, I need a copy of a royalty statement. With the notebook system, it's always right at my fingertips. And my agent and I frequently need to check something on a contract, so all I do is pull the notebook with the contracts off the shelf. I try to put everything in writing, so I like to keep my letters in one file that is always handy." Another freelancer describes her somewhat unorthodox system, one that nevertheless is ideal for her work as an editor: "My system is less casual than it used to be, but I still think you would say it's casual. I record what I earn every month in a little five-by-eight notebook. I fill in the date I was paid, the date I sent the bill, and a job description. I also keep copies of invoices on file. Then I save all my receipts so I can take the appropriate deductions."

At its most basic level, an accounting system shows how much money a business takes in as well as how much it spends. Most of the money coming in consists of payments for services, or accounts receivable, but a business usually takes in some other monies as well—interest on savings and investments, insurance reimbursements, royalties and licensing fees—and these must also be noted in your accounting records. The money the business spends, known as cash expenditures or disbursements, is equally important since the expenses of running a business are often tax deductible. All these receipts and expenditures are recorded in a systematic way so you can keep track of how the business is doing financially.

Since most businesses spend and take in money every day, they record their accounts payable and receivable daily. Some freelancers find they can do this weekly, if they do not have regular daily expenses and receipts. Examples of simple accounts payable and accounts receivable records appear on pages 92 and 93.

In addition, most businesses check or "close" their books once a month. This involves transferring the daily or weekly payables and receivables to a journal and then noting any irregular or monthly cash flows, such as electricity or a quarterly insurance payment, into or out of the business. This statement can then be reconciled, just as you reconcile your bank statement every month.

There are many ways, some already described, to set up the records for a freelance business. At its simplest, you could use a notebook to record accounts receivable and another for accounts payable. One file folder could hold copies of unpaid invoices; another could hold paid invoices. Duplicate files should be created for expenditures.

Freelancers tend to be casual about the money they spend. Often they do not even both with receipts. Because it's so easy to overlook small expenses, which nevertheless do add up, smart freelancers should keep a running pocket record of expenses. Small books for this purpose can be purchased in any stationery store.

One freelance illustrator has seen the wisdom of tracking even small expenses. "My accountant chewed me out last year and said I should write down my expenses every single day. She said I would be surprised at how much I spend. So I started doing it recently, and was I amazed. I spend a lot more on transportation than I ever thought I

ACCOUNTS PAYABLE

Date	Item	Place	Purpose	Account	Amount
6/14	Phone			Smyth	$11.80
	Cabs			Smyth	$12.30
6/15	Office supplies				$40.60
	Small office equipment				$10.00
6/16	Cab			Smyth	$6.80
	Bus				$1.50
	Lunch w/Don Smyth	Brew-It Pub	Discuss new assignment		$35.70
6/17	Air fare to Boston			ABC	$100.00
	Lunch w/Ned Jones	University Club	Discuss account maintenance	ABC	$18.00
	Taxis in Boston				$15.00
	Drinks w/Jennifer Chesler	Terminal Restaurant	Discuss reassignment of people on Dinnerstein account	Painter & Chatwin	$20.00
	Dinner	Terminal Restaurant		ABC	$10.00
	Taxis to and from airports			ABC	$35.00
6/18	Transportation to and from library		Research on Dinnerstein account	Painter & Chatwin	$3.00
	Office supplies				$5.00

ACCOUNTS RECEIVABLE

Date	Received from	Purpose	Amount
6/14	Smyth	Retainer fee	$800.00
6/17	Smyth	Payment for Ruddick, Inc., proposal	$1,200.00
	ABC	Payment for annual report (partial)	$2,000.00

did. I have always estimated it rather than keeping an accurate record. I deduct movies and admission to museums, but I never remember to save receipts. That costs me a lot more than I had realized." The illustrator is now a convert to frequent regular record keeping of cash disbursements, and you should be, too. If you can't face looking at figures every single day, then save the receipts and do them weekly.

Choosing a Record-Keeping System

There are many kinds of record-keeping systems, ranging from computer spreadsheet programs to simple "one-book" systems. The latter, records kept in one book, are satisfactory for most freelancers.

You can check out the one-book systems at your local stationer or office supply store. Ideal and Dome are two brands favored by many freelancers. Dome also publishes an Expense Account Diary, which is excellent for keeping track of your expense records.

As you get more involved with your records system, you may want to expand it, or you may need to expand it as your business grows. Additional files you might consider setting up and incorporating into your accounting system are:

Inventory/Purchasing:
   purchase order file
   supplier file
   receipts file for goods purchased
   stock file (needed only if you have an inventory)

Sales:
record of sales transactions file

Cash Records:
bank statement reconciliation file

Computer spreadsheet programs are another efficient way to maintain your financial records. Few programs have been adapted to specific businesses, but the more popular financial-management programs, such as Managing Your Money and Quicken, can be adapted to business use. These programs do on your computer what written record books do on paper, plus they reconcile your accounts for you. A spreadsheet can also be used to write checks, manage investments, and budget and forecast.

USING A CASH-FLOW CHART

Another very important financial tool is the cash-flow chart. Financial experts often downplay this in favor of profit-and-loss statements and balance sheets, but most freelance operations are too small to make much use of these, and every business benefits from using a cash-flow chart. As its name implies, the chart shows you how much money is flowing through your business, and that is exactly what you need to know to see how you are doing. It does not show profit or earnings but rather whether you have enough money to function. Some experts believe this is the most accurate way of measuring a business's progress. At least initially, you will be much more concerned with cash flow than with profit.

A cash-flow chart uses the money you have on hand, coupled with the money you are earning, minus your expenses, to show your net and cumulative cash flow. Net cash flow is obtained by subtracting the cash you take in from the cash you spend. Cumulative cash flow is obtained by adding the balance from the previous month to the cash in and then subtracting the cash out. A very simplified cash-flow chart appears on page 96.

The Profit Principle

Tracking cash is the most important function at first, but sooner or later you will want to look at profit as well. Some freelancers maintain that they have no interest in profit and are interested only in maintaining a certain lifestyle, yet every business, even a freelance operation, needs to earn a profit in order to survive. Profit is used to expand a business, as well as to give yourself bonuses. It is what carries you through the bad times when your earnings drop and you need another source of money to tide you over.

How much profit is enough? Every kind of business has its own profit range, although within that range there may be considerable variation, depending on the skills and creativity of individual owners. Very big corporations typically see profits of 4 to 5 percent, while many successful freelancers, who admittedly earn far fewer dollars, may realize profits of 50 or even 100 percent, depending on the business.

SETTING UP AND USING A BUDGET

Before you even start your business, you should begin drawing up a budget. Budgets are used to plan and forecast the future operations of the business. Unlike the cash-flow chart, which is based on real income, a budget is based on projected income. Budgets are not, however, fantasy documents. The only kind that actually works is a realistic one.

Particularly when a business is in the planning stages, it is a smart move to project earnings two or three years into the future, because it may in fact take that long to show a profit. Budgets are used in established businesses, too. Most owners draw up an annual budget and then check it monthly (or quarterly if your business is very simple) to see how they are doing.

A budget is above all else a planning tool. It helps you set a goal and move toward it. It shows whether you are making a profit. If you

CASH-FLOW CHART

	January	February	March
CASH IN Money fund Savings Checking Accounts receivable TOTAL IN			
CASH OUT Rent Utilities Office supplies TOTAL OUT			
Net Cash Flow			
Cumulative Cash Flow			

aren't earning as much net profit after taxes as you would be if you were working for someone else, then you are not successful financially, and you must do some serious planning—and to do that, you need to have a budget to look at.

Ideally, to do a budget you should know what your income will be, something that freelancers cannot always easily predict when they first start freelancing. After a while, however, you will begin to have an idea of what your yearly income will be. But before you know your yearly income, to plan a budget you must project your earnings, based perhaps on what you need to earn. For example, you can estimate that you will need to have three or five jobs monthly at $1,000 to $1,200 each in order to earn enough to live on. Based on this projection, in the absence of an earnings record, you can draw up a budget.

There are many kinds of budgets, but most freelancers can get by with a very simple one that shows whether they are operating in the red or the black. A sample for a very simple monthly budget is on page 97.

Insert your estimated taxes. Subtract the amount of estimated

QUARTER-YEAR MONTHLY BUDGET

	First month	*Second month*	*Third month*
Beginning cash balance			
Cash collection			

Cash payments
  Rent
  Utilities
  Operating costs			

Total net income before taxes			
Estimated taxes			
Balance			

taxes that you owe from the total net income, and you will have the balance. If the figure is positive—and enough for you to live according to the standard you like to maintain—then you are running in the black. If the total is negative or very small, then you need to figure out a way to earn more money.

One other kind of budget is necessary in order to analyze earnings. It shows actual and budgeted earnings and expenses. A simplified version is shown on page 100. At the start of every year, enter projected expenses and earnings. Each month fill in the actual figures and the variation, if any. If the variation is small, it is nothing to worry about. But, for example, if you projected that you would spend $400 a month on office supplies, and you are actually spending $600 month after month, then you have exceeded your projected budget. You are over by only $200 a month, but if this continues, you will be over budget by $2,400 at the end of the year. Depending on the size of your business and the amount allotted to office supplies, this is an overage you might not find acceptable. By using this kind of budget, you can keep a close eye on your earnings and expenses.

When Your Budget Shows a Deficit

When a budget repeatedly shows a deficit, something is wrong. It may be something you cannot control, such as the fact that the economy is headed into a period of inflation or recession. Even if you cannot do anything to avoid these circumstances, at least a budget allows you to see what is coming and take appropriate action. Most freelancers tighten their belts when they see a downturn in the economy. They know there will be less work and that they may be forced to use profits (savings) to get through a rough period.

When such a period is headed your way, you can take steps to minimize it. If inflation seems to lie ahead, you might order extra supplies now while they are still inexpensive or reduce or avoid unnecessary spending because you know costs are rising.

Budgets also show excessive spending that you *can* rein in. Do you really have to take taxis everywhere? Is there cheaper overnight mail delivery? You can pinpoint the exact area of waste or overspending and then take steps to cut back.

RAISING MONEY

Sometimes a budget shows that through no mistake of yours, the business temporarily needs more money to operate. You may have just completed a big job, but that client always takes two months to pay. Usually at such time, you do not need the kind of capital that is required to start a business, but rather a smaller influx to carry you through. Since freelancers have trouble obtaining bank loans, they often look to untraditional sources of money at such times. Here are some suggestions for doing this:

- Apply for a new credit card and take as high a line of credit as you can get.
- Take out a home-equity loan if you have equity in your home. This is a loan against the value of your house, and it can be very useful. You can use the money to support your business.

- Open a revolving line of credit at the bank. This should be available to you if and when you need it, but you should not have to pay interest on it until you use it.
- Arrange for similar loans from family or friends instead of a formal lending institutions. Be sure to draw up a loan agreement just as you would if you borrowed money from a more formal source.
- Don't rule out a bank loan. While bankers are not inclined to lend money to startup operations, especially freelance ones, they do not mind helping a successful business stay afloat. Your banker may be very inclined to give you a loan to tide you over in bad times, especially if it's just a temporary fix.

In seeking a loan, don't forget loan companies, insurance companies, credit unions, and commercial credit or sales finance companies. Finally, you can also ask someone to cosign your loan for you if you feel you will not be able to get one on your own to finance your business.

Do cultivate your banker a little before you request a loan. This may be easy to do if you live in a small community and know your banker personally. It is more difficult but hardly impossible to do if you live in a city. Don't just walk in one day and ask for a loan. Instead, talk to your banker about the kinds of credit that are available. Drop the fact that you run your own business and mention how well things have been going for you. Ask about business accounts and discuss whether you need one for your business. It is one of the great ironies of this world that bankers don't like to lend money to people who really need it, so you should sound self-confident and successful.

After you become acquainted with the banker, arrange for a meeting to discuss the possibility of obtaining a loan or a line of credit. Even if you are dealing with a neighborhood bank, don't show up for the meeting in cutoffs and a T-shirt. Look businesslike when you appear for the meeting. Have the papers you think the banker will request with you. Have a neatly typed copy of your business plan with you. If you have cultivated the banker's acquaintance, if you are well

ACTUAL AND BUDGETED EXPENSES

Budget This Month	Actual Expenses	Variation This Month	Budget Year to Date	Actual Year to Date

prepared, and if your income and credit rating qualify you, the chances are good that you will get the loan you need.

Your Credit Rating as a Freelancer

Once you have freelanced for a while, you should have little problem obtaining credit, provided your business shows a profit. (If it doesn't, again, why are you freelancing?) But in order to obtain credit, your credit rating must be sparkling. This doesn't mean that you have to be the promptest bill payer in town. Freelancers, like everyone else, experience cash-flow binds, and at those times you, like everyone else, will probably slow down paying your bills. The trick is to slow down on the bills that don't matter or get you into trouble. This varies from community to community. In some cities you can let the phone and electric bill go—that is, not pay it until you receive the next bill or pay only a few days before the next bill arrives. In other communities the utility companies are the first creditors to remind you that you have not paid promptly.

As a general rule, once you have figured out which creditors won't try to collect right away, pay off your big bills first and let the little ones slide. Occasionally pay off a bill before it is due. Paying off a loan early looks especially good on your record.

GETTING HELP FROM FINANCIAL EXPERTS

Many freelancers believe they do not earn enough money to seek professional financial advice, but the Consumer Financial Institute of Massachusetts says that anybody with an after-taxes income of more than $20,000 can use some. This goes double for someone in business for himself or herself. Many kinds of advisers are available, such as stockbrokers, lawyers, accountants, credit counselors, bankers, insurance agents, and financial planners.

Before hiring the services of any one of these people, though, think about who has the expert's loyalty. Many insurance agents, for example, earn commissions from insurance companies and as a result charge you nothing. This doesn't mean you don't get good—or free—financial advice; it just means the agent will be trying to sell you insurance along with the advice. His or her loyalty goes to the employer. On the other hand, you pay a financial planner or an accountant, and his or her loyalty is strictly to you. Both kinds of advisers can be very helpful, provided you understand the situation.

Before getting involved with any financial expert, check his or her references. The best reference, of course, comes from a satisfied client. You can also casually ask the expert the first time you meet about his or her background and training. Ultimately, though, before you trust anyone with your money, you should like the person. Personal chemistry accounts for a lot in choosing anyone with whom you will have financial dealings.

The one adviser a freelancer is most likely to have is an accountant or an accounting service. It is strongly suggested that you have an accountant do your taxes. In fact, if you feel you cannot handle the record systems that have been described in this chapter, you can hire an accounting service to set up a system for you. It is expensive; a one-time setup will cost $500 to $1,500. Hiring someone to maintain your books will cost a minimum of $1,200 per year. Some freelancers hire part-time bookkeepers to maintain their books for them, but this is expensive too.

Even if you maintain your own financial records, you may occasionally turn to your accountant for help. If you need to cut back on expenses, for example, but cannot see how to go about this, a consultation with your accountant may be in order. A good accountant should be willing to help you learn about finances.

WHEN YOU HAVE MONEY TO SPARE

Yes, with careful financial planning, the day will come when you have some extra money on hand. Your bills will be paid, your rent will be covered, and the work will still be coming in. For many freelance writers, for example, sizable chunks of money come in when they contract to write a book. When this happens, you need to think of something to do with the money between the time it arrives at your office and the time you need to start drawing on it to meet expenses. No small or large business ever lets money sit idle that could be earning interest, and your independent operation should not be an exception to this rule.

The easiest thing to do is to put the money into a savings account, where it will probably earn less than 5 percent. A smarter thing to do is to look for some kind of easily liquidated, high-interest place to put your money. Money funds are an excellent place to stash extra capital, and if you have enough money to meet the requirements for minimum deposits, you might consider a six-month certificate of deposit, commonly called a CD. Often, money funds and CDs require a larger amount of money than many freelancers can part with all at once, and you must lock up your money for six months or more. Before ruling these out, though, consider merging funds with a friend. While banks don't advertise this as a possibility, there are no regulations to stop you from banding together with one or more friends to pool your money for investment purposes. Just be sure you set up the arrangement in a businesslike manner and that you put your agreement in writing.

To learn more about how to invest money, contact stockbrokers, bankers, and other financial institutions. The advertisements in the financial section of a newspaper will give you many leads.

THE IMPORTANCE OF GOOD FINANCIAL HABITS

Many freelancers have a tough time understanding why they should take care of themselves financially. It seems to go against their grain in some way. Yet if you truly want to be a successful freelancer—and if you want the independence that comes from earning enough money to live well—you will concern yourself with financial matters. Many freelancers who have always felt they had no head for financial dealings are surprised to learn that they are adept at this once they learn what to do and how to do it. One thing is certain: If you want to be a successful freelancer, and that means anything from existing above a mere subsistence level to earning enough to live very well, then you must learn as much as you possibly can about the financial end of freelancing.

7

TAKING CARE OF NUMBER ONE

REMEMBER ALL THOSE BENEFITS YOUR EMPLOYER USED to provide and possibly even pay for, even if only partially? Health insurance, pension, retirement accounts? You must now make arrangements to provide these for yourself. In addition, as a self-employed person, you must now foot your entire Social Security bill, whereas when you worked for someone, you paid half and they paid half.

It is impossible to overemphasize the need to provide yourself with a solid and complete benefits package. Cost is always an issue, but you can buy what you can afford initially and then purchase more as your earnings increase. Starting out, you will need, at minimum, some kind of health insurance and a retirement plan. A disability policy is also strongly recommended.

RISK ANALYSIS: WHAT YOU NEED TO KNOW

How do you know what you need beyond this or how much insurance to buy? Risk analysis will help you determine this. No business is too small, or for that matter too large, to undertake some form of this process. Described below in eight steps, risk analysis begins with assessing your needs and concludes by telling you how to maintain the insurance policies you buy.

1. List all the ways you can possibly suffer loss.
2. List possible kinds of insurance. If you don't know what you need or what it is called, read on.
3. Talk to several brokers. It is worthwhile to shop around on insurance.
4. For convenience, try to find one broker who can provide several kinds of coverage. For example, one broker might provide renter's or homeowner's insurance, liability, and business interruption insurance. But if you find that buying from several brokers is cheaper than buying from one, then go that route. Also look for insurance sold by groups to which you belong. For example, one freelancer buys disability insurance from her university alumni group.
5. Do not conceal anything from the broker when you discuss your needs. This is silly and only hurts you in the long run.
6. Once you have policies, do everything possible to keep losses to a minimum to avoid the risk of cancellation. You do not have the protection you had when you were part of a large group.
7. Store your policies in a safe place, perhaps a safe or a lockbox. If you rent a lockbox for this purpose, it is tax deductible.
8. Review your policies periodically. Insurance is expensive, and it is worth your while to shop around not once a year but even more often. The owner of a small editing facility in New York City says he shops for health insurance at least twice a year and often cuts costs by switching carriers.

BUYING HEALTH INSURANCE

The most important benefit you can provide yourself is health insurance. This field has changed rapidly in the past few years as managed care has become the norm rather than the exception in the

United States. Rather than buying an individual health insurance policy, most people now join a health maintenance organization. Since managed-care organizations are committed to keeping health costs low, the advantage to joining one (at least in theory) is that you will spend less money on health care.

But there are also disadvantages. One is that you must select your physicians from a list of those who belong to the HMO. Another is that your gatekeeper physician, usually your internist, decides whether you need to see other specialists. You can either abide by his or her decision or pay for the doctor yourself.

Another disadvantage is that HMOs are not yet giving very good care outside their geographic regions, so be sure to ask what kind of coverage you have when you travel. If you don't feel you are adequately covered, consider buying a special travel policy.

The most expensive way to insure yourself is to buy an individual health insurance policy. You will be covered for any and all physicians you see, can choose your own doctors without concern for whether they belong to the same HMO, and will end up with a co-payment of 10 to 20 percent. These policies cost more than HMO coverage.

A few plans let you move between managed care and private insurance, with you picking up the co-payment whenever you choose to see a physician on your own, but these are typically expensive, employer-generated group plans that few freelancers have access to.

Keeping health insurance costs down is a constant concern to freelancers. One way to reduce costs is to purchase coverage through a group. Professional organizations, college alumnae groups, unions, and other similar groups offer group insurance to their members. Taking a higher deductible also can reduce health insurance costs. Most policies have a $200 deductible, but you can buy a policy with a $500 or even a $1,000 deductible. If you are reasonably healthy and confident that you will have the money to make up this difference, this is a smart money-saving tactic. Finally, as noted earlier, shopping around on health insurance on a routine basis is a good way to assure yourself of a competitive price.

TAKING CARE OF RETIREMENT

Once your health insurance is in place, the other important benefit that requires your attention is retirement. Most people do not begin saving for retirement until they are in their fifties. Although it is difficult to think about such things when you are in your twenties and thirties, time does have a way of creeping up on you, and the only retirement plan most freelancers will ever have is the one they fund themselves. Combine this with the vagaries of freelance wages, and it becomes doubly important for a freelancer to begin funding retirement as soon and as steadily as possible.

The sooner you start building a retirement account, the bigger it will grow. In fact, nothing speaks more eloquently about this than cold, hard figures. If you wait until you are fifty to sock $2,000 a year into a tax-sheltered retirement fund, assuming you manage to earn 8 percent over a twenty-year period, you will have saved only $132,000 for retirement at age seventy-one. If you start saving in the same manner at age forty-one, you will have sheltered $361,000 by age seventy-one. But if you start building a retirement fund at age twenty-one, your money will grow to over $2 million by age seventy-one. These are, of course, rough figures, unadjusted for inflation, that assume the money is tax-sheltered. Nevertheless, they give an idea of the importance of saving as early as possible. In addition to a retirement fund, most people have other savings.

A Word About Social Security

You already have one retirement fund, and that is Social Security. Social Security is a federally administered retirement-and-relief program that is available to every U.S. citizen. It is supported by taxes. In addition to funding retirement, it pays survivors' benefits to spouses, children, and elderly dependents of those who paid into the fund. It provides disability for long-term emotional and physical problems, under certain conditions.

When you worked for someone else, your employer paid about half the tax, but when you work for yourself, you pay the entire tab. Social Security taxes have been going up in recent years and will probably continue to rise as we begin to fund retirement for the baby boomers. Many freelancers find that with all their deductions, they end up paying more in Social Security taxes than in income taxes.

At present, Social Security retirement benefits are available from age sixty-two, with slightly reduced benefits, and from age sixty-five, with full benefits, although as the baby boomers reach retirement age, and worries grow about funding their Social Security, there is talk of raising the retirement age.

To qualify for Social Security, you must work a minimum amount of time, which is calculated in quarters, or three-month periods. It is a good idea to check your Social Security record every few years to be sure that it is accurate and up-to-date. It is especially important for anyone who is in and out of the workforce to do this. Women who drop out to take care of children, in particular, should track their Social Security with great care. Regional Social Security offices and post offices have a form to use for checking your records.

Retirement Accounts

Social Security was never intended to be anyone's primary retirement plan. Therefore, you need to set up an additional retirement plan.

The most common kinds of personal retirement plans available to freelancers are Individual Retirement Accounts (IRAs) and Keoghs. Your tax preparer or stockbroker can also advise you about kinds of retirement plans that may be available to you.

IRAs are available to many people who work and do not have other sources of pension funding, while Keoghs are designed specifically for the self-employed. Incorporated freelancers can shelter about the same amount in a corporate pension fund as in a Keogh. You can shelter $2,000 yearly in an IRA and, depending on your age and income, approximately $30,000 in a Keogh or a corporate pension fund.

IRAs and Keoghs were established in the 1970s so people could shelter retirement money from taxes. This is an enormous benefit. If you put the same amount of money in a taxable account, it would not grow nearly as much. Money in tax-sheltered accounts is not taxed until it is removed, usually at retirement age. You must begin withdrawing money from a tax-sheltered retirement fund at age seventy-one, and you may take out money as early as age fifty-nine and a half.

While money in Keoghs and IRAs is meant to stay there until you retire, it can be removed without penalty if you are disabled. In addition, Congress occasionally considers permitting IRA and Keogh money to be used without penalty for other reasons as well, for example, to fund college or to buy a first house. This may well happen at some future time.

IRA and Keogh money can be used for any reason if you are willing to pay a 10 percent penalty for early removal and pay taxes on the money. Making a decision to draw down a retirement account prematurely, however, should always be done with your accountant's advice.

Setting up a retirement account is no more complicated than opening a bank account. Money can be invested almost anywhere except in insurance policies, collectibles, and investments made with borrowed funds. When considering what kind of account to establish, look for safety and a steady yield over the years. Banks, brokerage houses, insurance companies, and investment management companies all offer retirement plans. Retirement plans can be either self-directed, meaning you manage your investments yourself, or managed by a professional, that is, an employee of the institution where you invest your money.

You will have to pay a setup fee and an annual custodial fee, but these expenses are deductible and fairly small, averaging about $50 per year.

A new plan must be set up by December 31 of the year in which you claim the tax deduction. With a Keogh, though, you can put money into an account any time until you pay your taxes, including any extensions you ask for, which usually means April 15 and August 15.

You can also switch your money from one account to another in order to take advantage of changing rates of return. This is called rolling over an account. You can roll over an account as often as you like if you send it directly from one institution to another. If the amount goes to you, you can roll over the account only once a year in this manner, and you must reinvest it within sixty days. Should you get into a cash-flow bind, this could be a way to get your hands on some ready cash—temporarily. You could have the money in your fund sent to you directly, use it until you get in the money you are owed, and then, providing you put it into a new account within sixty days, incur no penalty.

DISABILITY INSURANCE

The other important form of insurance that you should buy as soon as you can afford it is disability. A disability policy pays your salary if you are unable to work for a long period of time. It does not, however, pay for the occasional sick day. Far more people will be disabled over the course of their work life than will die, so in some ways it makes more sense to buy a disability policy than a life insurance policy if you can afford only one kind of insurance.

If you are unincorporated, as the vast majority of freelancers are, you are no longer eligible for workers' compensation, the government-sponsored disability policy. In addition, workers' compensation does not provide enough to live on, so even if you are incorporated and eligible for it, you will still need a good disability policy for fuller and more complete coverage. Freelancers are particularly at risk if something happens to keep them from working since they do not have an inventory that they can continue selling and there is usually no one else to run the business in their absence.

Some disability policies pay you only for the days when you are actually hospitalized; others pay for days when you cannot work. Disability covers you in the event of serious illness; it does not automatically pay you for occasional sick days as your former employer probably did.

There are several kinds of disability insurance, and you need to discuss them and your needs with an insurance agent. Disability insurance can sometimes be purchased through a group. One writer purchased a policy from her college alumni group that pays her $100 a day for every day she is hospitalized—another reason you are wise to look carefully at the benefits of any possible group you can join. She pays approximately $120 a year for this coverage. A therapist with a private practice spends nearly $1,200 annually for far more comprehensive coverage that would pay him one-half his salary should he fall ill. No disability policy covers more than a portion, usually one-half, of your income. This is because disability payments are not taxable.

Many freelancers put off purchasing disability because they feel they cannot afford it, and often they are correct if they want to purchase full coverage for their salaries. But if you want to find a policy that will pay your monthly bills and cover your rent, with diligent searching you can probably find some kind of suitable coverage. If you decide not to purchase disability coverage when you start freelancing, it is still something you should reconsider every year when you review your benefits package.

DISASTER INSURANCE

Disaster insurance is another important addition to your insurance roster, and since it is cheap, you should be able to purchase it from the moment you begin freelancing. Disaster insurance covers not only your household belongings and your actual household, but it typically provides some liability protection if someone is injured on your property. This can be especially important if clients will be visiting you in your home. Most disaster policies do not cover your business machines and equipment, but for a few dollars more you can buy a rider to cover these items. Disaster insurance is also called renter's or homeowner's insurance. The following list will help you buy—and maintain—this kind of policy.

- Try to buy as comprehensive a policy as possible.
- Especially try to get some kind of liability coverage; this is usually offered with a homeowner's or renter's insurance policy. If people will be coming to your home frequently for business

purposes, you may even need more than the minimal amount most renter's or homeowner's policies supply. Get as much liability as you can afford.

- Before buying a policy, find out how you will be compensated: (1) cash value of property at time of loss; (2) repair or replacement with goods of similar quality; (3) take all property at appraisal value or agreed upon value and reimburse you for losses.
- Even if you own several policies, you can collect on only one at a time. For example, if you own two renter's policies and you are robbed of $500 worth of goods, the policies will share the costs of your damages rather than each paying you $500. If you conceal or misrepresent property or try to make two policies pay for one loss, your policies may be rendered void, and you may have trouble getting this kind of insurance again.
- If you file a claim, take extra care to avoid future losses, or you may find yourself paying an unusually high monthly rate.
- When you do suffer a loss or damage, file immediately for damages.
- If you and your agent disagree regarding your losses, resolve them through appraisal procedures. In any event, you should have a list of what you own and even take pictures, if possible.
- If you have anything of unusual value, such as furs, jewelry, or antiques, you should have them professionally appraised and attach a special rider, which can be purchased for only a few dollars extra to cover these items.

As you become more successful, you may want to buy other forms of insurance. If you work outside your home, you will need specialized insurance to cover your office and/or studio. A variety of insurance policies cater to the needs of freelancers. You can buy the standard fire protection, but you can also buy business-interruption insurance to cover you in the event that your business is interrupted by fire, flood, or other disasters. Some policies are designed to cover you if your business is interrupted by lack of power, water, or heat. Key-person insurance can be purchased to replace the salary of an important employee other than the owner. In short, whatever your insurance needs, someone will probably sell you a policy to cover them.

With all the details of setting up a new business, too many freelancers let their benefits package become a secondary concern. This is a mistake. One of the best things you can do for yourself is to have a benefits package for yourself in place from the day you open your doors. If nothing else, it is one less thing to worry about.

8

FREELANCERS AND THE IRS

IT BEHOOVES A FREELANCER TO TAKE EVERY single deduction to which he or she is entitled regardless of whether the IRS approves. American taxpayers are entitled to do whatever they can to *avoid* paying taxes. What they cannot do—because it is illegal—is *evade* taxes. In this chapter, you will learn the difference.

THE IRS DEFINITION OF A FREELANCER

The IRS takes a dim view of all small, home-based business owners, believing that too many of us keep sloppy records and take deductions to which we are not entitled. They have sought for years to rein in freelancers. Various proposals for doing this have included placing a 10 percent withholding tax on freelance income, severely limiting the home-office deduction (more on this later), and tightening the definition of who is a freelancer.

Defining who is a freelancer is important and may even protect you when an employer tries to take advantage. In an attempt to avoid paying Social Security, unemployment, and workers' compensation taxes, some employers attempt to claim that part-time or even full-time workers are actually self-employed. And occasionally a bona fide freelancer veers into a situation that is nebulous.

Imagine, for example, that a client hires you for a very big job. You will work on it for several months or even a year or more. You will work in the client's office, using a computer he provides. It almost goes without saying that when you work in someone else's office even as a freelancer, you have less control over your hours and how you structure your work. Putting aside for the moment the whole issue of why you would allow yourself to have only one client, let's examine the tax implications of this situation. Are you still truly a freelancer? Or are you an employee and thus entitled to have your Social Security, workers' compensation, and unemployment taxes paid? The IRS doesn't like this kind of situation and can challenge your status as a freelancer if you are not truly functioning as one. Circumstances like this, in fact, have driven the IRS to clamp down on who is entitled to call himself a freelancer. To be considered a freelancer by the IRS, you must meet the following standards:

- You set and keep your own work hours.
- You control your daily work. This means you decide what you will do during the course of a work day rather than an employer telling you.
- You use your own tools and equipment.

Even if you meet this definition, the IRS may look more closely at your tax returns than those of non-self-employed persons, even year after year. Many freelancers find that the only way to deal with this is to adopt a zenlike attitude. Simply accept the fact that your tax returns will be looked at closely, then relax and live with this reality.

The good news is that the IRS can look as long and as hard as it likes, but it does not have to find anything. The best protection against an IRS audit—and the many hours of lost work this can cost you—is to provide the IRS with a neat, accurate, well-prepared tax return and then to back this up with equally tidy and complete financial records.

Paying Quarterly

Let's begin with the fact that you must pay your income taxes on a quarterly basis. This is required of all businesses, including freelancers. It requires a simple calculation. You estimate your tax bill for the entire year, divide by four, and make those payments, which are due on April 15, June 15, September 15, and January 15. Most freelancers grumble about how inconvenient the dates are, but most freelancers would not find any other dates any more convenient, and there is nothing you can do to change them, anyway.

On April 15, like everyone else, you figure out what you have actually made and settle up with the IRS, either by paying the remainder of what you owe or by getting a refund because you have paid too much.

If you do not file at all, you can be fined 5 percent of the tax due, up to 25 percent. If you file but do not pay, the penalty is considerably less—1/2 percent per month. (Both penalties are in addition to the 20 percent penalty for failure to pay quarterly or for underestimation of your quarterly taxes.) Occasionally, a freelancer who is in a cash-flow bind simply skips filing, but this is silly when you consider that the penalty for nonpayment is so much less than the penalty for nonfiling. This makes the situation regarding a freelancer's taxes pretty clear: Try to pay the IRS what you owe when you owe it because underpayment or failure to pay quarterly increases the size of your tax bill.

On the other hand, do not pay the IRS more than you owe. Because of the financial insecurity of freelancing, you may be tempted to apply an income tax return toward next year's tax bill. This, you think, will help to ease the cash-flow crunch that accompanies tax-paying time. It sounds like a good idea, and it may help you sleep better at night, but you pay a price for doing this. Someone is earning interest on money all the time. If you pay the IRS in advance or pay more than you owe, the IRS rather than you earns interest on your tax money. If you take the money from last year's return or estimate your earnings a little on the low side, then you earn the interest on that money. And you have the use of the money throughout the year.

Social Security Taxes and Freelancers

In addition to income taxes, virtually all taxpayers pay Social Security tax. This tax supports the government-mandated pension fund. (Chapter 6 explains in detail what Social Security does for you instead of to you.)

The Social Security tax used to be relatively small compared to income tax, but its rate has been climbing in recent years to the point where many freelancers now find themselves paying more in Social Security tax than they do in income tax. The Social Security tax bite is scheduled to increase for several more years.

As an employee, you paid only part of your Social Security tax, and your employer picked up the tab for the other half. Once you become self-employed, you are expected to pay your entire Social Security tax. To do this, you file a Schedule SE, along with your individual Form 1040, every April 15.

Why You Need Professional Help

By now you have probably arrived at the conclusion that you need professional help to file a business tax return. There are a couple of reasons for this.

One is that a tax preparer helps you get everything you have coming to you. Lots of freelancers think they will save some money by not using professional tax preparers when actually the reverse is more likely. Professionals know all the deductions, credits, and adjustments to which you are entitled and see that you get them. They know when you should write off new equipment and when you should depreciate it. They are current on new tax rulings and laws, which change frequently. They also help you interpret tax rulings, which can be so subtle that even individual tax preparers often give the same ruling different interpretations.

The other important reason to use a professional tax preparer is that this will help you avoid trouble with the IRS. Here's what can happen to a freelancer who tries to prepare his or her own income taxes: You figure you'll save a couple hundred dollars by preparing your own taxes. You are even something of a tax sharpie and pride yourself on having read a couple of books on the subject. You prepare your tax return yourself and file it on April 15, along with everyone else.

The computer spits out your return. It seems, as a startup business, that you have exceeded the IRS's projected spending range on office expenses. In fact, you have done nothing wrong. Most of your expenses were one-time charges related to setting up your new office, and the clerk who looks at your return understands this.

But then he sees that you have filed a fairly complex tax return without the assistance of a professional tax preparer. (Tax preparers must sign returns along with individuals.) Smelling blood, the clerk decides it could be worthwhile to go on a hunting expedition. Even if you got this one thing right, there is a good chance that you made a mistake somewhere else on the return. Before you know it, you are in for a full-dress audit—all because you insisted on saving a few bucks by doing your own tax return.

Overall, your best bet is to find a good accountant or tax preparer—possibly even one who freelances. Finding the right person can be tricky, and many freelancers have horror stories. Some report their accountants' reluctance to let them deduct their home offices, even though they have no other base of operations. Another freelancer notes that the first accountant he saw let him deduct almost nothing and insisted that he open a retirement account before he would handle his taxes. Another freelancer's accountant refused to let her deduct her home office because most of her mortgage payments were interest, and he said this would be a double deduction. It might be, if *all* the payments were interest, but that was not the case. There was something left over, and she should have been deducting a home office. These few examples should suffice to convince you that you have to know a little about your tax situation even to work with an accountant. You don't want someone who plays so fast and free with your money that you are frequently audited, nor do you want someone who discourages you from deductions you have every right to take. You do want someone who knows every single loophole and who will encourage you to reduce your tax bill in every possible way. It's a nice bonus to find someone who can give you some basic financial planning advice as well.

Resist the notion of hiring the sleaziest possible tax preparer, who you are sure will save you even more money than a straight arrow. There is one big problem with this. The IRS knows all the problem tax preparers, and preparers, as noted earlier, are required to sign the returns they prepare. With a sleazy or even an incompetent tax preparer, your chances of being audited escalate. Furthermore, your tax preparer sometimes goes with you when you are audited, so you want a reputable representative.

Presumably, this can all work in reverse, too. If you hire an accountant who has a flawless reputation with the IRS, he or she is less likely to encounter close scrutiny since the IRS knows from years of seeing his or her returns that they are well done.

By the way, it's perfectly reasonable to question any tax preparer you are thinking of hiring about his or her audit rate. A really good tax preparer will not have an audit rate higher than 10 percent, nor will he or she have one of 0 percent. At 0 percent, you are probably faced with someone who is too conservative.

Now that you see why you should not deny yourself professional tax advice, here is some advice on how to find the right tax preparer:

- Word-of-mouth is the best way to find a tax preparer. Satisfied people love to pass on the names of their accountants.
- Get someone who does returns for lots of freelancers, preferably in your field. That means, if you are a writer, get an accountant who works with a lot of writers; if you are an artist, get an accountant who works with lots of artists.
- Ask the accountant for his credentials when you make the initial phone call. Find out what professional associations he belongs to. Remember, though, that he need not necessarily be a certified public accountant, a credential many people look for, but he should be an enrolled agent, certified by the IRS to prepare taxes.
- Find out what she charges and how much time she thinks will be required to do your taxes.

WORKING WITH AN ACCOUNTANT

Once you have found an accountant, there are some things you can do to make his and your work easier. For the kind of attention you need, you will probably pay an accountant by the hour rather than on retainer. In small rural communities, this hourly fee to prepare a business's taxes runs from $40 to $80; in large urban areas, it often runs $150 to $250. Therefore, it is to your advantage to reduce the amount of time you spend with your accountant, and you should also have some idea how much time your accountant expects to spend on your business. Shelley Martin, an enrolled agent and a senior partner at Weickart Tax Associates, which does thousands of returns for freelancers and small businesses in New York City, reports that one to two hours is the average amount of time she spends on any one job, although once she spent eighteen hours on a very complicated job that required a great deal of research. Martin notes, "When someone shows up and dumps a year's worth of receipts on my desk, I tell him to go right home and sort them out himself because he will only pay me for the time I spend sorting out those receipts."

Sort your own receipts *before* you go to the accountant. You need not even take them with you; just take a list of the totals for your deductions. For example, note your monthly rent on office or studio space, how much utilities are, how much you have spent on office and other professional supplies, how much on entertainment, and then take these totals to the accountant's office. If you are not sure whether an item is deductible, take the figures anyway and let your accountant advise you.

YOUR DEDUCTIBLE, ADJUSTABLE LIFE

A very important way that freelancers reduce their tax bill is by taking deductions and adjustments. Although there are technical differences, for practical purposes the primary difference between the two is where they go on your tax return. Business deductions go on the Schedule C. Business adjustments, like personal adjustments, go on the 1040 form.

There are also tax credits, but these are of little value to most small-business owners at this point. Credits have by and large been replaced with adjustments to income.

Before getting too carried away with deductions, remember that for every deductible dollar you spend on your business, only about one-third is actually saved in income taxes. In addition, not all expenses are fully deductible. You can write off only the portion of your home that you actually use for business, for example. Entertainment is not fully deductible the way it was for many years. If you combine business and personal travel, only the days actually spent conducting business are deductible. And the IRS has some really stringent rules about travel.

Below is a list of deductions typically taken by freelancers:

Rent or mortgage payment for office or studio
Utilities
Real-estate taxes on property used as office or studio
Depreciation on office or studio if owned
Travel for business
Education
Transportation
Membership dues
Publications, newspapers, journals, etc., related to your work
State sales tax
Safe-deposit rental, if you keep business papers in it
Retirement plans
Moving expenses
Subcontracting
Clothes, if worn specifically for work
Tools and supplies needed to carry out work
General office supplies, including business stationery and cards
Postage
Answering service and/or machine

Office equipment
Depreciation on office equipment
Bad debts
Public relations and advertising expenses
Gifts and holiday cards to clients
Legal services
Financial planning services
Entertainment
Insurance
Repair services
Equipment or furniture rental
Printing and copying services
Cleaning services and/or supplies

The Home Office Deduction

The home office has long been one of the more controversial deductions. Basically, the IRS views it, at least for those with deductible mortgages, as a double deduction. A few years ago, the IRS clamped down with some tough new restrictions and a public announcement that it would audit everyone who deducted a home office. One restriction required that a home office be located in a separate room that could not be used for any other purpose. Obviously this caused a genuine quandary for the countless thousands of urban freelancers who live in small apartments or, even more so, in studios.

While the IRS was forced to back down on the separate-room restriction, its point was made when it came out on the right side of a Supreme Court decision. The case involved an anesthesiologist who did all his case preparation and maintained all his patient records in a home office. The Court found that his real work was done in the operating room, and that he was therefore not entitled to a home office deduction. At present, for a home office to be deductible, it must be used exclusively as an office, and it must be the place from which the majority of a freelancer's income is generated.

This means a home office is still okay for most artists and writers.

But one may not be okay for an author who earns the majority of his income lecturing or for a restorer who does most of her work in someone else's house, even if she maintains a studio in her home.

Some tax preparers no longer let their clients, even the ones who are entitled, take the home office deduction. Others permit their clients to take it but attach a note explaining the deduction, a gesture that is tantamount, according to Shelley Martin, to waving a red flag in front of a bull.

There is another lesson in this as well, and that is that the IRS, at different times, looks askance at different deductions and adjustments. Every year at tax time, there is a lot of talk about "safe" and "unsafe" deductions. Yet deductions are not so much safe or unsafe as they are in favor or not in favor, à la the home office deduction. The best solution is to rely on professional advice. It is your tax preparer's job to know what the IRS is looking at or not bothering with.

The Health Insurance Adjustment

The IRS has only recently permitted freelancers to take their health insurance as an adjustment on their income, even though this has long been a deductible expense for incorporated businesses. As of this writing, 30 percent of health insurance can be deducted from your income.

The Social Security Tax Adjustment

Social Security has long been a deductible expense for corporations, which pay and then deduct half the expense for their employees. Only recently, though, in a long-overdue recognition of the fact that freelancers are indeed small-business operators, has the IRS allowed freelancers and other unincorporated small-business owners to take a 50 percent adjustment of Social Security on their income.

The Bad Debt Deduction

Freelancers, who are hurt much more than big businesses by non-paying clients, commonly assume that they can deduct the cost of a bad debt. But you can deduct a bad debt only if you claim the income on your return and pay taxes on it.

The Education Deduction

The education deduction is another often misunderstood tax break. You cannot deduct classes intended to help you find another job or retrain into a new career, but you can deduct educational expenses that help you maintain or improve the skills you already have. An artist who works in stained glass can take classes in stained-glass technique, for example, and a business consultant can deduct psychology and business classes taken to maintain his or her business expertise. But the stained-glass artist cannot deduct business courses he plans to use to retrain as a business consultant.

KEEPING UP-TO-DATE ON TAXES

If you insist on preparing your own taxes, be sure to avail yourself of one or more good tax guides. These are usually annual publications, so they are current on tax rulings. Although they are not specialized by profession, they can give you a lot of general background information. Computer tax programs are similar, except they are software that enable you to use your computer to calculate your taxes. For freelancers, they have the same disadvantages as tax preparation books, that is, they are not really specialized enough to help with most businesses.

Please note, though, that while the outstanding tax preparation program has not yet been invented for most freelancers, a computer spreadsheet on financial management is an excellent way to keep track of your financial records. At tax time, all you have to do is print out the year-end summaries and take them to your tax preparer.

KEEPING RECORDS

Ironically, the IRS does not specify which records you should have if they audit you. At a minimum, save your checkbook register; receipts payable, accounts payable, and/or a general ledger; all specific expense receipts; your appointment calendar; and any correspondence relating to insurance claims and late payers.

An excellent and neat way of tracking your expenditures is to use a credit card, especially a card designed for business purposes. Some credit card companies now offer a business card (usually for a bigger annual fee) that provides year-end summaries of expenditures, broken down by category. If you don't want to flip for a separate card or pay the big annual fee, then enlist with a credit company that supplies you with a year-end tote sheet, and separate out the personal from the business expenses yourself. Or maintain one card that you use only for business.

You can also track your business expenses on computer. Quicken and Managing Your Money are two time-tested software programs designed to track annual expenses. They are geared to household rather then small-business use, but often these programs can be adapted to business use.

If you maintain your finances on a computer, take care to pull regular printouts of the general ledger as well as the checkbook register and to back up disks regularly. The IRS does not want to hear that your computer destroyed your records any more that it wants to hear that your dog ate them.

TAX PLANNING: WHAT YOU CAN DO

Too many freelancers believe they are such small operators that they cannot do anything about tax planning. And while it is true that you probably will not have extra cash lying around to invest in pork bellies on the commodities market (a notoriously easy way to lose your money, by the way) or even in blue-chip stocks, there are things you can and should do to save on your income taxes. You should use your money in ways that spell tax savings for you. The first and most obvious thing is to make sure as much of your life is deductible as possible.

One book editor, who experienced several lean years before start-ing to earn a comfortable living, made deductible living her philoso-phy of life, albeit in a small way. She reports, "When I started freelancing I knew I was going to have to give up some luxuries I had been used to when I had a regular paycheck every month. Even things I had taken for granted, such as going to three or four movies a week, were now reconsidered. I decided that books, a deductible item for me since I edited fiction and nonfiction and had to keep up with the marketplace, would become my major luxury. After all, they were deductible. When I couldn't stand not spending any money friv-olously, I bought myself a book. When a few checks came in and I felt rich, I rewarded myself with a book. I could just as easily have gone to a movie or treated myself to an expensive dinner, but I knew the book was deductible and the movie or dinner wasn't."

This freelancer's instincts were right: She opted to spend her money on deductible items where possible. That is the first step to saving money through your taxes. There are other ways to make your life deductible. When you take a vacation, see whether there is some way to combine it with business. If you are a writer, find a subject you want to investigate or someone to interview at your destination. Dancers, musicians, and artists can visit galleries and studios and can talk to people about working for them. When you combine leisure travel and work, be sure to write letters in advance requesting ap-pointments so you have proof of actually having conducted business.

You can also plan the timing of your deductions. If you want to pur-chase a new computer, for example, and you have a choice between buying it in a year when you earned a little and a year when you earned a lot, it will be more helpful to your tax situation to buy it in the year when you earned a lot. You will end up paying fewer taxes on your greater earnings.

Another way to increase your deductions is to pay for items in advance. Pay your January rent in December, for example, if you need another tax deduction. Just don't forget that you cannot claim this payment on next year's income.

Many freelancers try to micromanage their income the same way they do their deductions. Toward the end of the year, they attempt to push off income into the next year. A common ploy is simply not to cash a check that is received in the last week or two of the year until the new year. Another is to ask a client not to pay you until the new year. There are several problems with this. One is that the IRS expects you to claim all income you receive in the year you receive it, even if the check arrives in your mailbox on December 31. The other is that your clients will be trying to pay you this year so they can deduct you. The solution that offends no one is to ask the client to cut your check on the last day of the year. He gets the deduction for that year, and you receive the check in next year's mail.

Also keep in mind that manipulating your income this way can ultimately backfire on you. In a successful business, your income continues to grow every year, so by putting off income, you are simply making it larger for future years. It's better to plan to pay your taxes when they are owed.

WHAT IF YOU ARE AUDITED?

The worst has happened: The IRS has called on you to come in and discuss your return—in short, you are being audited.

Keep in mind that the chances that this will happen to you are not really very great. The IRS audits a very small percentage of the general population. Because you operate your own business, you may be at slightly greater risk.

Understanding how people are chosen for an audit also will help you to see why you are not likely to be audited. The IRS has a computer program that establishes norms for deductions in each income category. For example, if you live in New York and earn $40,000 a year from freelance income as a design consultant and you spend $10,000 on entertainment, that probably is more than the norm for your occupation and income category.

What happens? Your return will be kicked out of the computer. But merely being kicked out of the computer does not mean that you will be audited. It means that your return will be looked over by a clerk, who then flags your return for an audit or passes on it based in part on how much money the IRS is likely to get if it audits you. For example, more audits are done among people earning over $50,000 a year than among those who earn $20,000 or less. This does not mean, however, that if something is glaringly wrong on your return you will not be audited just because you do not earn very much. If there is something wrong with your return—if a deductible category is unusually high for no apparent reason—the IRS will question you about this and possibly conduct a full-scale audit.

Tax experts know that several things trigger an audit or cause the IRS to question some part of an income tax return. In a sense, you already do one big thing: You freelance. And since you are not about to stop freelancing simply to decrease your chances of being audited; there is no reason to do anything else to decrease your chances. If for some reason you have high expenses in one year, and they are fully receipted, deduct them even if they cause you to be audited, which they probably will not.

What other things increase your chances of being audited? If any of your deductions are abnormally large, you may be called in for questioning or possibly an audit. If your income tax refund is high compared to your income, if you work in a business where you could easily be hiding a lot of income, and if you cannot live on what you appear to earn after deductions, then you are a likely candidate to be audited. But all this is a matter of common sense.

If you are going to be audited, it will probably happen one to three years after you file a return. In 2003, the IRS will be auditing returns from filing year 2001. There is a six-year statute of limitations on false or fraudulent returns involving 25 percent or more of your annual income. There is, however, no statute of limitations on filing an intentionally fraudulent tax return or on failing to pay on over 25 percent of your gross income. This is why most tax preparers advise clients to keep their income tax records forever.

If you are called for an audit and you can justify your deductions, then you have nothing to fear. Consider the case of the architect who moved his business and residence from Florida to New York. The first year he claimed net earnings (after deductions) of $16,000 and a deduction of $7,000 for entertainment expenses to establish his business. He was called for an audit, whereupon he produced detailed receipts covering his entertainment expenses. He walked away unscathed since all his expenses were so well documented. Only when your expenses are not documented do you have anything to fear from the IRS. Simply having a large deduction may be enough to get you audited, but it is not enough to get you in trouble with the IRS.

If you are called for an audit, there are a few things to keep in mind:

- If at all possible, schedule the audit for your tax preparer's office or your office. If your office is in your home, definitely opt for your accountant's office or the IRS office. Most of the time, the audit will be held in the IRS office; that is the usual practice for a small audit.
- For your own peace of mind, don't postpone the meeting. Get it over with as quickly as possible.
- If the IRS letter does not specify what areas of your return are being considered, call and ask. Then take only the records that relate to that area with you. Walking into an IRS audit with all your records when you are being questioned about only one area is an open invitation to the auditor to escalate the audit. If your business equipment expenses are the area in question, take only the receipts for your business equipment expenses and nothing else. If business equipment and entertainment expenses are being questioned, take only those receipts.
- If you are being audited for something relatively minor, you may not even need to take your tax preparer with you, but if you sense trouble (if your deductions are not well documented) or are especially nervous when faced with authority, then by all means

be sure she accompanies you. In fact, she can go as your representative, but since your affairs are under discussion, you would do well to accompany her.

- Dress nicely but not richly. If suitable, wear the clothes you wear to work.
- Be polite and straightforward to the agent.
- Do not act defensively; you may only appear cocky. In fact, do not talk a lot or try to make small talk. The agent cannot be warmed up to your interests, and he or she is fully aware that you are nervous.
- Arrive on time.
- Make sure your records are neatly organized. Throwing a bundle of loose receipts on an agent's desk will only annoy him; it will not stop him from meticulously sorting through them with a vengeance. After all, he has all day.
- Only answer questions. Do not ask them if you can avoid it, and whatever you do, do not volunteer any extra information that might open up another area of your return for audit.
- You need not show your working papers or notes to the agent, which does not mean he won't say, "Here, let me take a look at those." If you are easily intimidated and might hand over your notes, this is all the more reason to have your tax preparer along with you. In fact, if you have an accountant in tow, the IRS agent probably will not even suggest such things as looking at your notes or reviewing other nonrelated areas of your return unless he has planned in advance to ask you about those areas.

Official IRS publications remind taxpayers that audits are not necessarily anything to be afraid of. The IRS initiates an audit because it wants to verify information on your tax return, not because it is out to get you. And many audits come out in the taxpayer's favor—that is, you may walk away with a little more money than you had to start with.

It does not make good business sense for a freelancer to avoid taking a deduction or to take less than you are entitled to because you are afraid of an IRS audit. The real trick is not to be afraid of the audit.

Handling the Mail Audit

Your chances of getting a letter from the IRS adjusting your tax bill are far greater than your chances of being audited in person. Such letters usually come from the general offices of the IRS, not the offices where auditors work. You are told what changes are being made in your tax bill and are invited to: (1) sign the letter and remit the amount in question, or (2) respond in writing with an explanation.

One freelancer received a letter from the IRS stating that she had underrepresented her income by approximately $5,000 and asking her to remit an additional $1,500 in taxes and penalties. Once she recuperated from the shock, she began to go over her records. Since she knew she had not underpaid her taxes by that or any other amount, she soon found the IRS's errors and wrote a letter explaining why she did not owe that amount. The IRS sent a return letter acknowledging her explanation and accepting it.

Many freelancers are so intimidated by the IRS that when they receive letters asking for smaller amounts, they are often so relieved that the amount is small and that they are not being audited that they readily remit the money. Never let yourself be intimidated so easily. Anytime the IRS questions you about any amount, no matter how large or how small, double-check your records to see if you really owe the amount. Never sign or agree to anything until you have checked it to be sure the request is accurate. The IRS can and frequently does make mistakes, and many of those mistakes are on freelancers' tax returns, which may be a natural result of the fact that their returns are not so routine as the average taxpayer's are.

Taxes and Talking Shop

Taxes inevitably are a favorite topic of freelancers, like everyone else, especially around April 15. While there are some benefits to be gained from comparing notes on your tax situation or on possible deductions, you are better off not discussing the specifics of your individual tax situation with anyone. Freelancing, like any business, is competitive, and in some creative fields, the competition becomes intense—and a friendly competitor just might decide to turn on you. One particularly hostile way to do this is to report anything you have said to the IRS, which does have paid informers. Annually the IRS has about seven thousand paid informers, who earn an average of $700 each. Most informers are exes—ex-wives, ex-husbands, ex-friends, and ex-colleagues. Obviously, there are trusted colleagues with whom you feel confident discussing your tax situation, but in general remember that what people do not know about you, they cannot use against you.

GOING TO TAX COURT

If an audit goes against you, you can sue the IRS. Before you do this, though, you are entitled to an immediate review by your auditor's superior and a further written appeal within the IRS.

After this, you can appeal in tax court or in U.S. district or claims court. The tax court holds sessions in approximately a hundred cities. There is even a small-cases court procedure. The amount in question must involve less than $5,000 in one year. You can represent yourself, and you cannot appeal.

Keep in mind, though, that citizens who sue in tax court rarely fare well. In small-cases court, for example, citizens win a clear-cut victory only about 8 percent of the time. The IRS wins outright about 53 percent of the time, and the rest of the decisions favor both parties. Judges are especially tough on taxpayers who file what they consider to be frivolous suits. To cite just one example, insisting that you will not pay any taxes unless you can designate your tax dollars for environmental causes definitely qualifies as frivolous.

In summary, it sometimes helps, when dealing with the IRS, to keep in mind that you are not more vulnerable to the IRS as an individual but because you operate your own business. If you run your business in an aboveboard fashion, seek out good advice, and then follow it, you are probably no more vulnerable, as the operator of a freelance business, than Mr. or Ms. Average Citizen.

9

SELLING YOURSELF

SELLING YOURSELF IS THE HARDEST PART OF freelancing, as every freelancer interviewed for this book agreed. No one likes to do it very much, and many freelancers dread it. It's a special bugaboo for new freelancers, who feel insecure and scared in general about their new ventures. But when you freelance, you are the product. Often you are the only thing you have to sell—and with few exceptions, such as those freelancers who have agents or representatives—you are the person who does the selling. Take heart, though. Selling yourself does get easier once you have learned how to do it and as you gain experience. And fortunately you will build up repeat business and also begin to get referrals, which means you can spend less time making cold calls and soliciting new business.

DEVELOPING THE RIGHT ATTITUDE

In order to sell anything, you need contacts. These are either prospective buyers or leads toward prospective buyers. In this chapter, you will learn how to find your customer, whatever service you are selling, and you will learn how to sell yourself to that customer.

The methods most commonly used to sell are personal contact, advertising, and display. Since freelancers essentially sell services, display—as in decorated windows and flashing signs—are of little use. Advertising helps somewhat, depending on the nature of your business, but if you are on a tight budget, you can probably get along without it or spend very little on it. Advertising is discussed in Chapter 13. The sales method most frequently used by freelancers is personal contact. You call or write someone. You personally solicit business.

One advantage of the personal contact method of sales is that it is cheap, especially for the new entrepreneur who may have little else to do with his or her time. It costs very little to make a phone call or mail a letter. An appointment that lasts twenty minutes is, relatively speaking, an inexpensive sales pitch.

Although freelancing does depend on personal contact, this does not imply intimacy. Too many freelancers come on like puppies, indicating a willingness to chat about anything and everything on the phone, having forgotten their days in an office and how overcrowded they were. Often, too, the new freelancer, feeling a little isolated and having trouble getting used to the days alone, is unnecessarily hurt when someone does not have time to talk or abruptly ends a meeting or phone conversation. Don't let yourself fall victim to these feelings. Keep in mind the days when you worked in an office and viewed phone calls and meetings as unnecessary interruptions of your busy day. Friendships can and probably will develop between you and some of your clients (one of the pleasures of freelancing is the open-ended opportunity for finding and making new friends), but this will happen over time. Meanwhile, as a new freelancer, it is more important for you to learn how to accept and maintain the degree of professional distance you need to run your business. Suggestions for doing this are also discussed later in this chapter.

When you first begin selling yourself, it will seem very strange to you. Making and using contacts is like your first day on a new job, except that this is something you will have to do over and over throughout your freelance career. At first your goal will be to establish contact and to try to build a working relationship. Your ultimate goal, though, is to get work, or possibly to get an appointment to discuss future work.

In a sense, freelancing is just the opposite of working as an employee. As an employee, the longer you work for someone, the greater your chances of staying on. As a freelancer, you do not have this security. While you will have regular customers who use you over and over, each job is new and separate from the last. And since the employer does not have to fire you but can merely stop calling you, as a freelancer, you are always being tested. Bill Cook, a playwright who freelances as a typesetter, remarks, "If you freelance, you have to be very good at your job. If you're very good at it, then you keep working. You're not let go when other people are. And even if an employer really doesn't like to have freelancers working for him, he'll keep you on." Freelance editor Sharon Kapnick comments, "I think you have to be really good. I try to treat each job as if it were the first job—and the only job—for a client, and as if my life depended on it."

FINDING CLIENTS

If you are thinking about freelancing, you probably already have an area or profession in which you will work. More specifically, though, when you begin to seek work assignments, you have to pinpoint which persons or companies are likely to need the specific services you offer. When one woman decided to switch from teaching to freelance editing, her long-term goal was to write for textbook companies, but she correctly sensed that this was not an entry-level position, even with her teaching background. After talking with freelance editors, she decided that her best bet was to solicit copy editing and proofreading. She then turned to *Literary Market Place*, the bible and phone directory of the publishing industry. She also studied the ads in *Publishers Weekly* to see which publishers were likely to need freelance copy editors. She called trade-book publishers first and was quickly rewarded with several assignments. Eventually, as her business and her self-confidence grew, she began to approach textbook publishers for copy editing and proofreading. As she built her contacts in that area, she began to talk to them about doing some writing. That kind of work came in slowly, but she was eventually given an assignment to write some exercises for lower-grade workbooks. That led to still another assignment. She found that her new area of expertise was growing, thanks to referrals. Her success, though, is largely attributable to the fact that she found the right place to enter her field, pinpointed a list of prospective clients, and went after them rather than wasting her time (and prospective clients' time) with a scattershot approach.

Another freelancer, who went through a similar experience when he started, makes this suggestion: "Sit down and write a paragraph describing your prospective clients—who will need you and why, how often they will need you, who will be best able to pay you well. Then turn to trade directories and publications and use your own contacts to find those potential employers."

Barbara Zimmerman, at one time the only person in New York to freelance in copyrights and permissions, worked hard to carve out her niche after she had settled on publishing as the general field in which she was qualified to freelance. "I don't know where I found out that nobody did what I do freelance, but I decided permissions and copyright was a possibility. I started by writing a series of 300 to 400 letters to publishing houses. I followed up with phone calls. Basically, everyone said no, we don't buy this, our staff people do it. We don't need it. And then everyone had an emergency. Everybody assured me that this was one unique emergency and that there would be no more business. They all became steady clients. I've worked for everybody again except one client. That's how I got in the door."

Sally Chapralis had her own way of finding clients when she started: "I called all the people I could think of in the field, starting with all my former employers' competitors. I began there, not as any retaliation to my employers, but because I assumed that the competitors would feel that I specifically had something to offer them. I sold myself, and it worked. I also used the grapevine to find out about possible clients whenever I felt comfortable doing so. Mostly, though, apart from the initial calls I just described, I went in cold."

Whether you are looking for clients or for a special area in which you might sell your services, here are some places to conduct your search:

- On-line databases, including the Web. The largest and fastest-growing source of information on all subjects is on-line databases, such as Compuserve and America Online, and, of course, the World Wide Web. In these information networks, you will find job directories, often tied to specific industries, job listings, résumés, and a host of other work-related information. The best way to find out what's available for you is to join a professional forum, where you can chat on-line with others who do what you do. Most professional organizations, such as the Society of Journalists and Authors, maintain their own Web pages, which are another source of information. Anyone looking for any kind of freelance work will regularly, and perhaps even predominantly, use this source.
- Public library. Libraries have lots of vocational information, and you may uncover some special area you had not considered.
- The local chamber of commerce. These people can tell you what is going on in your community, where demand is greatest and lowest. This works especially well in a small community.
- Universities, particularly ones where you have studied. One freelance librarian got his start by simply mentioning his intention to freelance to the dean of his school. That was three years ago when he was completing work on a master's, and the dean is still diligently referring clients to him.
- City and state government agencies. Like the chamber of commerce, they can help you find your niche based on your community's specific needs.
- In recent years, many communities have begun sponsoring small-business development agencies, which can be very helpful to freelancers. Check your local telephone directory or library for more information about this resource. Small-business development centers have also sprung up in many universities. These agencies provide excellent expert advice to small-business owners.

- Field offices of the Small Business Administration. Most offices have retired executives, members of the Service Corps of Retired Executives (SCORE), who are eager to help you in your new venture. Call your regional office.
- The U.S. Department of Commerce. It doesn't have anything like SCORE, but it does have an interest in supplying you with information about any areas that you may be investigating for their freelance potential.
- Field directories and guides. They are too numerous to list here, but just to give you an idea of what is available, here are a few possibilities. In advertising, *The Creative Black Book* is the "telephone" directory, so to speak, of the business; in publishing, people use *Literary Market Place;* museum workers refer to the *International Directory of the Arts* or the *American Art Directory;* librarians use the *American Library Directory.* There are also any number of annual handbooks and periodicals that provide information about and sources of freelance work. *R.N. Magazine* for nurses advertises hospitals' personnel needs throughout each issue, and it also publishes an enlarged edition that is an annual review of nursing positions. Writers can choose from the sources listed in *Writer's Handbook, Writer's Yearbook,* and *Writer's Market.* Comparable books are published for commercial artists, designers, and photographers.

  Most libraries have a copy of the *Foundation Directory,* which contains information about more than 2,500 foundations; it is a useful tool for anyone who plans to solicit work or grant money from them. The list for all freelance careers is too specialized to cover here, but explain your needs to a librarian and don't be surprised when he or she produces a book that lists potential clients. It's that simple. If you can afford to buy the book, it may be a worthwhile investment. Sometimes, as with *Literary Market Place,* published by Bowker, you can order the book from the publisher; at other times, you may have to join a professional organization to get a directory. The point is to find the books, annual special issues of magazines, periodicals, guides, and directories that apply to your business. Ask others who do the kind of work you do, and check with your local librarian. Regardless of how specialized your area is, there are guides and directories that will help you.

- Colleagues. Most freelancers will not pass along their active clients, but they will share inactive clients or general leads ("Call Bill Smith; I hear he needs freelancers now") with someone who is just starting out. Also use this as an opportunity to find out what it is like to work for various clients. Freelancers love to share this kind of information and will be very honest with you.

- Catalogs and sales sheets. If possible, get this information from prospective clients, from the chamber of commerce, or the library. This way, you can pinpoint the kinds of services a client is likely to need.

- Your own survey. This takes a little nerve. Call up potential clients and ask them if they ever use freelancers. Jack Sharp, a freelance typesetter who was looking for areas into which he could expand his business, decided that employee handbooks were a possibility. He further decided that small manufacturing companies might be a prime target; they were too small to have advertising agencies who did this work for them and were large enough to need employee handbooks. Most were union operations, too, another reason they would be interested in publishing a guide to employee relations and benefits. He called twenty small manufacturers and found out that five were definitely interested, twelve had no interest at all, and three wanted to talk more about it. Those numbers represented a high level of interest to Sharp, who wanted to handle only four or five of these projects a year to supplement his other freelance typesetting. For him, a survey resulted in sales.

LETTING CLIENTS FIND YOU

As your freelance practice builds, clients will begin to come to you, and you can look forward to making fewer and fewer sales calls to prospective clients when you do not have a name you can use to get you in the door. Ursula Beldon, a successful set designer who has always freelanced, says she eased into this situation right after school, although she acknowledges that going to the right school in her field helped immensely: "I made contacts at Yale and got my first assistant's job before I graduated. It's all word-of-mouth in my business. You do one job for someone who likes your work, and that person recommends you to someone else."

A freelance indexer says, "Now I occasionally get jobs where my name has come up thirdhand. Someone I worked for told someone else, who in turn, without knowing me, passed my name on to yet another person. I used to start looking for new work as soon as I was finishing a job. In the last year I haven't had to do much looking on my own."

One therapist in private practice recalls, "I have one client who was recommended by the sister of an ex-client. That sister lives in London, and she gave my name to someone who was coming back to the United States. Then I have what I call my great-grandchildren among clients—friends of friends of friends, or third-generation clients."

It is important always to have a network of people—friends, acquaintances, colleagues—who can refer clients to you. You should do this in a low-key manner, though, but keep in mind that people like to help others. If your work is good, which it must be anyway for you to survive, then friends and acquaintances will be delighted to recommend you to prospective clients. One person whose freelance business consists entirely of ghostwriting books for others notes, "Referrals are the only way I get work." Robyn Cones, a freelance masseuse, has built her business entirely on referrals. She notes, "My business is all by referral. I can't advertise because of the nature of my business. I tried it just once and got too many loonies."

Joining Professional Organizations

There are several things you can do to help clients find you. The most obvious is to join professional organizations and groups where you will meet others who may need your services. Often these groups publish directories of their members, and anytime you can be listed in a directory, you are liable to pick up some extra business. But directories will be only a small portion of the business you will receive through your professional activities. For the most part, just mingling with other group members will be enough to build your business.

Speaking of the kinds of contacts he builds through professional associations, freelance librarian Bryan Johnson comments: "Solicitations for freelance work are very informal, and you often don't even realize you've been offered the job until you've already been interviewed—say, at a professional meeting or even at a social gathering. You need to project an image of self-confidence all the time. You have to believe in yourself. I'm never obvious at a professional meeting. I keep a high profile, though. I always mention to people that I freelance. I often find that people are more interested in my freelance work than in my regular job."

The first step, then, is to join any and every professional group or organization that could possibly be a source of clients or client referrals. Don't, however, join a group without first considering what it can and cannot do for you. It is important not to waste time on a group that isn't right on the mark in terms of what it can do for you professionally. Sometimes this is easier said than done—finding just the right group takes effort. Michael Tucker, a freelance business consultant, remained a member of a group of professional builders because his last employer had been a contractor and he had always belonged to that particular group. Eventually he took stock of his situation and realized that he had gotten very little business from the group and that in fact most of his business came from architectural firms. He began attending meetings of a group of professionals who worked in architecture and soon was getting more referrals than he could handle.

Whenever you are thinking of joining a group for professional reasons, consider the following:

- The number of members. Is the group large enough to be a viable source of contacts for you?

- Who the officers are. Are they real movers and shakers in your field? If so, that is a good sign.
- The benefits offered by the group. You may even find yourself joining a group with which you have only tenuous professional connections because it provides a benefit you need and can't get elsewhere.
- The yearly dues. Some professional groups are prohibitively expensive to those who are just starting out. Don't join if you really can't afford the dues; you'll only resent the membership later.
- What the group has accomplished. You should join only groups that are highly respected by the persons who hire the people in the group. Associating yourself with a group that has a reputation for being flaky or disorganized won't help build professional contacts.

Professional Subscriptions

In addition to joining groups, it is important to subscribe to and read professional trade publications in your area as well as in related areas. Their advertisements can be an excellent source of freelance contacts, and they also enable you to keep your eye on developments in the profession. Trade magazines also provide information about movement in the profession, sales and mergers, new acquisitions, and trade shows where you might contact new prospective clients.

MAKING THE INITIAL CALL

As you go about the business of selling yourself, remember that the first calls are the hardest. And to be totally honest, it is a rare freelancer who actually enjoys soliciting work. There are two kinds of calls: cold calls and calls where you do, in fact, have a connection, however tenuous it may be. Most initial calls are made by telephone.

The value of having a connection may be overrated, as many freelancers have discovered. You personally may obtain a feeling of legitimacy when you have a name to use as you make a call, but its real value has yet to be proved. And consider this: If you are diligent about making cold calls, following up with a letter and then yet another phone call, you may find that you have achieved the same kind of rapport by the third or fourth contact that you would have if you had a connection.

Set designer Ursula Beldon offers proof that making cold calls frequently does pay off: "If you don't have the right contacts in the theater, but your work is really good, you can sometimes get through to designers for assistant's work by calling on them to show them your portfolio. I got my present assistant that way. He sent me a résumé in the mail, and I needed someone, so I met with him and liked him and hired him. It wasn't all that smooth—actually, he had kept in touch with me through several phone calls. But I was a cold call on his part."

A freelance business consultant says, "I write or call people out of the blue. I don't mind writing letters, but I hate making phone calls. I've learned, though, that if I'm not successful right away, often I hear from people ten months later. It works out in the long run, but I don't like the phone work. It makes me feel awkward. It helps to know that I'll get some work. It makes it all seem less futile."

One freelance writer offers this hint on getting yourself motivated enough to make cold calls, or for that matter, any kind of sales calls: "I try to set aside one morning a week when I know I have to build up my business. I usually pick Friday morning. I do it because I plan a reward for myself when I'm done. Sometimes I have a nice lunch with a friend. If I have the time, I go to a movie or even take the entire afternoon off."

When making initial sales calls, either by phone or in person, remember that first impressions count. If your phone personality is abrupt or unpleasant or if you don't present yourself well, then you are less likely to get a job than is the freelancer who takes care to make a good first impression.

If you are nervous about your ability to carry things off, practice what you are going to say or role-play with a friend to make sure you present yourself well. When you do make a call, avoid putting on a formal voice or manner. Keep small talk to a minimum, especially on the phone. Because you are home all day, you may find yourself in a chattier mood than usual when you do call someone. Remember that the person at the other end is in an office and won't necessarily welcome idle chitchat.

Speak in your most pleasant voice. Don't interrupt the person you talk with, but be prepared to end a long awkward silence, perhaps by asking some questions about the kind of work the company does or about some detail of his or her work. Act enthusiastic; remember you initiated this entire process, so you are the primary person who wants something. A little enthusiasm goes a long way when you are soliciting business, but don't brag; if anything, err on the side of humility. But if you are asked to describe your work experience, which you almost surely will be, then be specific about what you have done even if you don't want to name clients. If at all possible, though, float the names of a couple of your major clients in front of the person you are talking to. Prospective clients are often reassured to know who else has hired you. And even a loose tie is okay to use. One enterprising freelancer always claims a major airline as one of his past clients, although he had been subcontracted through another freelancer to do some work for the airline and never worked directly with it.

Records of Your Calls

As you make calls—cold or otherwise—and as you call on people, you will need some record of this activity. One freelancer reports on her method of keeping track of her calls: "I keep a small file box with index cards. On one side of the card, I write the vital statistics—company name, address, name and title of person I have to talk to, kind of work I might do for them, who suggested I call, and so on. On the other side I note the date of the call and what we discussed. I don't write much, but what I write is very meaningful. Because I check in with someone only every month to six weeks and I may never have met him or her, I note when I called and the exact date when I'm supposed to call back. If we happened to discuss anything personal, I make a note of that. For example, one person I work with is crazy about cats, so I have a note to that effect. Another person is an aspiring opera singer in her free time, so I have a note about that. These notes help me place the person, and if the occasion does arise for a little small talk, I have a hint of what to talk about." A freelance artist's representative has a similar system, and she also adds small brightly colored metal clips to her cards, coded to the week or month when she wants to make a follow-up call. A photographer's representative carries a small notebook that contains an index card for each advertising agency, where it is located, and what work his photographers have done for it in the past.

Another freelancer who had worked for a highly organized man acquired his habit of keeping a detailed log of all phone calls. She said it paid off the only time she had to threaten to sue someone. She had put in several hours on a project, which the client had later canceled and then had refused to pay her for the work she had done. Her ability to cite details of their dealings, including his verbal commitment to her, caused him to render payment rather than risk a legal suit. Many freelancers work on a casual basis that does not include contracts or confirming letters, so keeping a phone log is an excellent idea.

Regardless of how you make your initial contact, your goal is to obtain some business or to build a solid enough relationship so that you will be called in for future assignments. Successful contact has been made when your skills and talents match the needs of your prospective client. Sometimes you just get a lucky break, as one young aspiring costume designer did. After weeks of calling an established costume designer about the possibility of working as an assistant, he finally connected with the woman on a Saturday afternoon. She told him she was working in a theater and could meet with him briefly there. He headed over, sat down, and chatted with the woman for a few minutes until she said, "Well, when can you start?" Thinking that he was being very eager, Jackson replied, "How about Monday morning?" The designer one-upped him, however, by saying, "How about right now?" He became a costume designer's assistant that afternoon. This freelancer admits that he had laid his groundwork for his lucky break, having previously sent samples of his work and having diligently called the designer back every single time he was told to do so. He does attribute their finally connecting for what turned out to be a long and happy association to his luck in thinking to pick up the phone on one particular Saturday afternoon, when he thought he just might catch the designer in her studio at a relatively quiet time.

Part of making contacts requires knowing when to give up. Sometimes someone just does not have any business for you and never will but doesn't come right out and say it. Sometimes, as photographer's representative Barbara Lee learned, you just have to have a second sense about when to quit. She comments: "I have no special technique for getting through to a prospective client. There's no courtesy on their side. They never call me back. I just keep calling until I get hold of them. Either they're busy, or they're away from their desks, and there are plenty of $200 a week secretaries and receptionists who don't want me to make a living. I do have some sense that anyone who has treated me really badly won't want to see my face again. If someone stands me up, for example, I just drop it. I now can feel where I'm going to get work and where I'm not. I know where to push and where not to push. I'm very persistent, but there is a time to call it quits."

THE FREELANCER'S RÉSUMÉ

The subject of making contacts also brings us to the subject of the freelancer's résumé. There will be occasions when you will be asked for a résumé.

A freelancer's résumé should never run more than one or, at most, two pages. Ideally, get everything on one page. Put your title—Writer, Editor, Typesetter, Set Designer, Actor—at the top of the résumé. A sample of a freelance editor's résumé is on page 149. Because there are so many areas in which people freelance, it is impossible to print representative sample résumés, but the one that follows shows generally how to describe freelance business. In some professions, such as acting, set designing, or dancing, a résumé is unnecessary, but in many fields it can serve as a sales tool— subtle advertising, as it were.

JOHN DOE, III
EDITOR/REWRITER

481 West Barry Street   Telephone: 312-555-8670
Chicago, Illinois 60657

Areas of Specialization

Social sciences, particularly political science and psychology; business; adult education. Secondary and college levels.

Experience

I have worked on all levels of textbooks and have a strong production background. My editorial and production skills include developmental work, writing and rewriting, and copy editing. Am also experienced in public-relations writing.

Clients

McGraw-Hill   Bols (Brown Foreman Distillers)
St. Martin's   Simon & Schuster
M. Evans   Graphic Alliance, Inc.

Employment History

April 1991 to present: Over six years ago I began my own editorial services business, supplying various clients with a variety of production and editorial services.
October 1988 to April 1991: Project editor, Madsen Textbook Publishers, Inc. Worked in social sciences and adult education.
October 1987 to October 1988: Senior editor, Flynn Publications. Worked in social science.
June 1986 to October 1987: Associate editor, Flynn Publications

Education

B.A., University of Iowa, 1986, education

SELLING IN PERSON

Telephone calls often eventually lead to appointments to see people who can offer you work. An appointment is important, something that you should prepare for carefully. The rules for a freelance appointment are much like those for a job interview, which after all is exactly what this is. Here are some pointers:

- Dress appropriately. Wear something comparable to what you expect to find the person who interviews you wearing. Later, when you are working for someone, you can pop in and out of the office dressed more casually, but for a first call, dress like a professional.
- Take samples of your work if suitable.
- Show that you have done some homework by talking intelligently about the company needs and how it might put you to use.
- Be prompt for the appointment. You may be kept waiting, but you should always be on time.
- Be prepared to meet several people. If the person you meet with likes you, he or she may want you to meet others in the company. Always go to an appointment prepared to meet more people than the one with whom you have set up an appointment. So allot extra time just in case. You don't want to miss your chance to meet the president of the company because your dentist is expecting you in ten minutes.
- Ask what specific jobs are coming up and find out whether you will be considered for them. Be a little brazen about presenting yourself as the person for the job. This is not the same as bragging. Rather, it is the age-old technique of closing the sale. If you don't say, "Well, that certainly sounds like an interesting project, and I would very much like to handle it for you," that may be the only reason you don't handle it. Ask for what you want—the worst that will happen is you will be told no. And that kind of no is hardly a permanent no; it merely means that you are not considered right

for this particular job or that it has already been promised to someone else.

- Finally, one woman discussed one more aspect of the freelance interview that was echoed by many other freelancers. It has to do with a kind of tension that often exists between those who freelance and those who do not. She notes, "I try not to appear too thrilled with my life when I call on someone. There's a freelance mentality about that. I think that sometimes the people I work for would like to do what I do, but they're not secure enough to do it or they're afraid to do it, so they don't want to know or think that the grass is greener on the other side, so to speak. They don't want to know that I can afford to go to Europe or California."

CREATING REPEAT BUSINESS

Once you have made your calls, had an appointment, and finally gotten an assignment and completed it, the next phase of handling your contacts is follow-up. Handling this stage can be tricky, and your technique will vary from business to business. One thing tends to apply to all freelancers, though: You often have to follow up, or you may not be called again. Yet, even if a company is eager to use your services and uses you almost constantly for several months or even a year or longer, the day will come when the work slacks off. It doesn't mean you won't ever get any more work from this client; it just means you are in a period of "staying in touch." How regularly you stay in touch and the means you use depend on your personality and that of your clients. For everyone, though, the trick is to keep your finger on the pulse of your client's operations without becoming a pest. This may mean a weekly call; it may mean a monthly call. It may not mean a call at all but might require a letter.

Follow-up is a very low-pressure kind of sales work. A good guideline is that as soon as you get any concrete information about when a client will next have work for you, jot it down on your notecard or whatever you use, and then don't call back until it is time to check on that specific assignment. Tell the client you will call a couple of weeks before that date to check on the assignment so he or she knows that you have not vanished. You no longer have to waste your time on phone calls, nor will the client dread the morning mail or the ringing of the phone because it might be a particular freelancer for whom he or she has no work at the moment.

Once you start getting repeat business, your life will become immeasurably easier, and your self-confidence will soar. One longtime freelancer says this is exactly when he solicits new business. "I always make calls for new work when I'm busy with present work. For one thing, I think I look more desirable if I say that I'm busy at the moment, but I just wanted to introduce myself and let them know that I'm available. I think clients talk more freely about future projects because they know I'm not desperate for work. But mostly it's good for my ego. It doesn't hurt at all and can even be fun to call prospective customers when you're feeling good about yourself because you've got a full in-basket."

When those repeat business calls and letters do start, here are a few guidelines for responding.

By Phone

1. Answer your phone promptly. If your telephone is answered electronically, make sure the call is answered right away.
2. Say "hello" or your name. Either is perfectly businesslike. You can use your company name if you have one, but consider how this appears to people when it is clear that you are the entire business. In some businesses, this is fine, while in others it's a little impersonal, and even pretentious.
3. Write down the substance of all phone calls. You will get many assignments over the phone; the phone log is a good record to have.
4. If you have more than one line or call waiting, dispense with additional incoming phone calls quickly but politely. Don't ask people to hold but rather say that you will call them back right away.

5. If you need to look up some information, ask if the person waiting wants to hold on or be called back. If you know you cannot put your finger on the information right away, then say you will have to get back to the caller.

By Letter

1. Your letters should be businesslike and friendly, yet not overly chatty.
2. There should be no typing errors.
3. Indicate your intentions clearly in the letter. Never beat around the bush.
4. Put as much as possible in writing without offending a client or making him think you do not trust him. Remember you need not confirm by letter in a formal way. You can just drop someone a line in which you happen to mention the assignment, fee, and due date.

GETTING ALONG WITH CLIENTS

There is an art to getting along with clients. On the one hand, freelancing offers many opportunities for making new friends, and freelancers often become friendly with the people they work for. After all, there is no employee-boss relationship here, so that barrier does not stand in the way of friendship. As one employer says, "It helps to become friends with the freelancers you work with. I try to. The more you can communicate to people about what you want, the better and easier it is for everybody. I don't have to give orders. Everything happens on a very pleasant basis in which I ask questions and supply answers, and vice versa. It's a very cooperative venture."

It is also important to realize that there can be a negative aspect to the looseness of the freelancer-client relationship. At least until you learn to establish some authority, you may be walked over by clients. One successful freelance editor says, "Many editors, even senior ones, act as messengers. And they don't charge for it. I sometimes deliver the finished product to meet the editor, but I don't act as a messenger. I make my connections, but once I've made them, unless we both need to talk with the manuscript in our laps, I don't pick up projects. Editors do, all over town. It shocks me. You get treated as you behave, and this is one of those little things that is very important. When someone asks me to do something I don't consider professional, I say, 'Gee, I wish I could do that.' That's a nice phrase to remember."

Another freelancer reports, "People try to waste my time. They want me to come in and talk before they've shown me the work. I always say, 'I can't tell you anything until I've seen the project.' Sometimes someone refuses to mail or messenger originals, so then I say, 'Fine, I'll come down in a cab and charge you for it and for my time.' They usually quit right then. What they're really angling for is to save a messenger fee, and once they learn they can't do it, they start behaving."

Sexual Harassment and Physical Safety

As a freelancer, you probably thought you would never encounter sexual harassment again. Well, think again. The reality is that freelancers, especially women, encounter it as frequently as regular employees—and are often more vulnerable when they do. Many freelancers do work that puts them in some degree of physical danger. Real estate agents, for example, earn a living by making appointments with strangers and then meeting them in empty apartments. But many other freelancers—masseuses, personal trainers, therapists come to mind here—are at risk as well. In fact, anyone who goes into a stranger's home to work, or worse, lets a stranger come into her home, needs to think about personal safety.

The first step is to recognize the danger. Denying it only leaves you more vulnerable. Many freelancers underestimate or play down the hazards. Jody, a personal trainer, was nearly raped by a client before she recognized the perils of her work. The client, an executive with a résumé so impressive she didn't bother to ask for references, gave her trouble the first time they met. After their session, he asked her to wait a minute while he went into his bedroom to get his checkbook. A few minutes later, he sauntered out unsuitably undressed and came on to her. Used to handling the occasional client who thought she might be interested in supplying something more than physical training, Jody explained that she was not interested, that she had a boyfriend.

Although she felt a tug about scheduling another session with this client, she did, because like most of us she needed the work. Should trouble arise, which she thought was unlikely based on her experience, Jody felt she could handle it. After all, she was stronger than virtually all her clients, including the men. Their second and third sessions went well. On their fourth, just as she was letting down her guard, he accosted her. She fought him off and managed to flee. Although Jody was physically unharmed, the emotional toll was not so minor. She felt stupid and demeaned and now found herself anxious about new clients. With hindsight, Jody saw that she should have heeded the first warning. Since then, she has carefully checked the references of all new clients.

Sharon McIntosh, a real estate broker who works in Manhattan, weighed the potential danger she faced and made plans to protect herself before anything happened. When she heads out for an appointment, she leaves her schedule behind with an assistant. Like many real estate salespeople, she knows all the doormen, and when she brings a new client into a building, she makes sure to greet them in the client's presence and sometimes even introduces them.

Dealing with sexual harassment calls for different strategies. For starters, freelancers cannot complain to their superiors. Most corporations have enough trouble dealing with the charges leveled by their regular employees. They back away faster than the speed of light when these accusations come from a contract worker.

In addition, as a freelancer, you may need to keep the offender as a client. Obviously there are times when you cannot afford to do this because you might be putting yourself in physical danger, but the freelance editor or graphic designer who encounters sexual harassment is more likely to try to deal with the situation than to dump the client, at least initially. Fortunately, it is easier to do this at arm's length than when you have to encounter the offender every day at work.

It's also important, as McIntosh points out, to recognize the difference between the client who is simply looking for a date and one who intends to wield sexual power over you. The former she handles more deftly, warmly assuring him that while she is flattered by his attention, she is married and unavailable. The attentions usually stop, she says, and she keeps the client.

The sexual harasser, however, is not seeking a date. He expects sexual favors in exchange for giving you work. This kind of client usually has a repertoire of tricks designed to make freelancers feel vulnerable. He can ask you to pick up a work assignment at his home. Or he can insist on an evening meeting and then try to turn the occasion into a date.

He also needs to do something to keep you involved, since unlike a regular employee, you can walk away at any time. One insidious and fairly common ploy is to criticize your work while still dangling the possibility of an assignment. The scenario goes something like this: Your work isn't quite right. Well, you ask, what you can do to make it right? It turns out he is happy to show you, on his own time no less. As you move through this delicate little dance, the assignment becomes more and more coveted, like a gold ring you can't quite grasp. You keep reaching for it, just missing it by a little bit each time, by his reckoning. And so it goes, until you finally get the message. More than your professional skills are required here.

If you find that otherwise acceptable work has suddenly become substandard for one client, who for some strange reason is still willing to hire you, be alert to this kind of hidden agenda. Ninety-nine percent of the time the problem is not your work.

What can you do when this happens? The safest strategy is to avoid situations where you are vulnerable. Always turn down inappropriate or offbeat proposals. A boss would not usually expect you to deliver work to his house, so there is no reason to do so for a client. Refuse all suggestions to have dinner or otherwise meet with him outside the office. Even if you would normally dine with a client, if you suspect an unwelcome interest in you, decline all such offers and politely but firmly insist on meeting with him in his office.

Make it clear that you are available only during regular working hours. If a client calls you at 7 P.M., announce that you are eating dinner or putting the kids to bed. Offer to call him back "during regular business hours tomorrow." (And if clients regularly call you at all hours, then you are a candidate for a separate business telephone.)

If the harassment continues or escalates, you may need to handle it more directly. Once your dealings reach this stage, you probably will not salvage the working relationship anyway, but then why would you want to? Sometimes, it works to call the client's bluff. Ask someone who is picking apart your work why he would want to hire you if he considers your work inferior. Or simply end the charade. Tell the client if you are not given an assignment by a specific date, you will assume he is not going to hire you and stop wasting his and your time.

If you believe this person still might be useful as a contact, that he might, for instance, pass your name along to others whom you might want to work for (stranger things have happened), then some tact may be called for. Simply say that you have unexpectedly gotten very busy and will not have time to do any work for him right now.

If the situation has deteriorated to the point where you no longer care to have any contact, it can be very healthy to vent your feelings and let the client know how you feel. This can be a powerful way of redressing the imbalance. Finally, keep reminding yourself that you do have power in situations like this. It stems from the fact that you are not an employee. And in the overall scheme of freelance life, that's worth a lot.

WORKING IN SOMEONE ELSE'S OFFICE

One of the trickier situations freelancers encounter are those times when they are asked to work in an employer's office. This is a situation rife with both petty and not-so-petty problems.

Regular workers often resent the freelancer who is free to come and go as he or she pleases or who may work only a partial day or only part of the week. There is little you can do about the resentment you encounter except remain congenial and perhaps occasionally point out that there is a downside to freelancing as well, if you can remember what it is while your are working in someone else's office.

A bigger problem is the unclear line of authority that emanates, or rather, does not emanate, from a freelancer. Freelancers don't exactly have bosses, and they aren't exactly bosses either. Much confusion results from these acts. The smart freelancer initiates a conversation with the client to clarify the situation as quickly as possible. If you are in charge of other workers, then they should be informed by the person who hired you. And then you should proceed to act like a boss if that is what you were hired to be.

Even when these situations are dealt with, many freelancers report that they still end up feeling like inferior employees. Sometimes even small distinctions help, as Sally Chapralis observes: "When I have worked in other people's offices, it has been my experience that when I am actually on the payroll, as opposed to freelancing out of their offices, then my status is lower. I am regarded as a part-time employee, so to speak, and although I have had some authority and status, it wasn't as much as I had when I have freelanced. This kind of limbo is not as psychologically rewarding as having my full independence as a freelancer or being a full-time employee. It is up to the freelancer to establish that mood and her status immediately. If you do that, you won't have any problems working in someone else's office." It also helps to learn to assert your authority. Bryan Johnson does most of his library work in other people's libraries, and he reports that he had to learn to establish his authority in order not to waste time: "I'm much better now than when I started. At first, I tended to be too grateful, almost groveling. Now I'm not terrible about it. I don't barge in and start rearranging furniture, but I let clients know in a fairly strong way that I will need a typewriter and a desk or workspace. I make sure they know they have to provide these for me. I don't go in like gangbusters, but I don't act mousy either. If they didn't want the work done, they wouldn't have hired me. If they want it done right, I need these things. I rarely have trouble now that I've learned to be stronger about these things."

LETTING SOMEONE ELSE SELL YOU

If all else fails, and you really hate selling yourself and do not do a good job of it, then think about hiring someone to sell you. Persons who sell the services of others are called agents or representatives. There are two times when you can quite legitimately use a sales agent: (1) when it is the custom in your trade, as it is with almost all authors, photographers, craftspersons, and artists, and (2) when you can't face selling yourself.

The one hitch is that there are some industries where you will simply be laughed out the door if you send in a sales agent. But even then, you can sometimes circumvent trade custom. In New York City, a group of copy editors, indexers, and proofreaders banded together and hired a sales representative/office manager. Although the group eventually disbanded for other reasons, it was accepted while it existed.

In almost all freelance professions where agents are the custom, the agent or rep takes 15 to 40 percent, depending on the field and the kind of arrangement that is standard. To get a reading on what you will pay, ask other people in your profession what they pay their agents.

When looking for an agent, try to find someone who has the following traits:

- Good business sense. After all, this is the part of your work that you are hiring him or her to handle.
- Sense of organization. If you can't stand this part of the job, now is your chance to get someone who is good at it.
- Handles others who are like you. For example, a large agency is not the place for a beginning author, however much you may be seduced by its reputation. Get someone who will pay personal attention to you. This applies in every field where agents are used.
- Good sense of follow-up. Good agents are always one step ahead of their clients. They call you about prospective work or a bill that is due to you before you have a chance to call them.

The very best way to get an agent—perhaps the only way—is through word-of-mouth referrals. Once you have the name of someone who might represent you, arrange a meeting if possible. In sizing up an agent, trust your instincts. This person will know a great deal about you financially, and your earnings will be based in large part on his or her ability to sell. If you like the agent, chances are that other people will, too.

Finally, here are some pointers on getting along with an agent:

- Get a contract, if that is customary in your field, spelling out what each of you owes the other. Some fields, such as music and publishing, are exceptions. Musicians do not sign with an agent, even though he or she may be working for them, until a third party has offered a contract. At that point the musicians and agent draw up a contract with each other. Between literary agents and authors, there is also often no contract, although increasingly today agents are asking their clients to sign letters of agreement.
- Learn the etiquette of your business and follow it. An author's money, for example, always goes to his or her agent; that is a sign of friendly relations between the two. These are the little things you need to know when you start working with someone.
- Keep your agent posted on your business dealings. For example, if you run into some prospective business at a party, inform your agent. Don't make any deals without your agent—she is there to negotiate for you. Remember, that is why you hired her. Never undermine your agent by negotiating on your own. The best way to avoid ever being in this situation is to say, whenever the subject of money or contracts comes up, "You'll have to talk to my agent about that."
- Give your agent any information, sales tips, or pointers that will help him sell you, but spare him details he does not need. Most successful agents are busy people; therefore, any information you can give about how to sell your services will help. One writer always considers her attempts to help her agent successful when she sits in an editor's office and hears him describe

the sales potential of her book in the same words that she has spoken earlier to her agent. Your agent, on the other hand, does not need to hear how difficult a time you are having researching something or exactly why you need fast payment for a finished project.

- Settle your agent's fee and then forget it. Your agent, strictly speaking, is an independent entrepreneur just as you are. She does not work for you as your employee. She will, if she is any good, work very hard on your behalf and completely earn her commission, so it is only good manners to be gracious and thankful to this colleague and not to begrudge her what you pay her.

- If things are not going well between you and your agent, talk about it and possibly end the relationship. Never gossip about your agent to others, especially people in the same business. Word of your dissatisfaction might get back to your agent and make him or her work less hard for you. If you are unhappy with your agent, fire him or her *before* you hire a new agent.

It is a rare freelancer who truly enjoys selling himself or herself, but this is no reason to be inept at selling. Like it or not, it is a major part of your work life. Fortunately, selling is a skill that can be learned. If you feel you need some help in this area, take a course or find a seminar or assertiveness training. It will be money well spent.

10

ALL ABOUT FEES

TOO MANY FREELANCERS EARN LESS THAN THEY might because they do not push for as much money as they are worth, nor do they negotiate as well as they should. One freelance dog walker, a veteran of fifteen years as a freelancer, who could easily command 30 to 40 percent higher rates than he does, started low and has never raised his prices much. He is, by his own admission, "simply too timid to look someone in the eye and demand a substantial increase." It's a situation you needn't find yourself in.

FIGURING OUT WHAT TO CHARGE

It is hard to figure out what to charge. Freelance fees in all fields tend to be idiosyncratic. Rarely can a freelancer set an across-the-board price for services. Most freelancers, like it or not, have sliding fees. Some old, favored clients are always charged less than newer, more affluent clients. Some clients are charged overtime and for rush jobs, while others never are. And in almost every field freelancers charge different rates for corporate or commercial work as opposed to creative or literary work. A set designer reports that he does television commercials only because they pay so much more than his theater work. He notes, "I can use one successful commercial, on which I earn royalties, to subsidize two off-Broadway shows each year. I want to do the off-Broadway shows because people in theater see my work, and because it's creative. I don't get as much satisfaction from the commercial work, but I do get paid well."

Then, too, there are various ways to structure a freelance fee. In the course of the year a freelancer is likely to take on jobs that pay by the hour, by the day, and by flat fee. Those who work in publishing have even more ways to charge: by the page, by the line, by the number of rewrites.

What does it all mean to someone starting out in freelancing who is unsure what to charge or even how to figure out a fee schedule? Basically, a freelancer should not get too caught up in working for one preset fee—for example, for one hourly rate. Sometimes you take a commercial or consulting job that is not particularly interesting or challenging but that pays well, so you can later take on creative work that does not pay so well. The trick is to charge enough overall so that you earn what you need to earn. But even a sliding scale or a willingness to negotiate does not mean that you will not require a well-planned rate schedule. If you go into a meeting to settle a fee and are unsure what to charge or what you would like to earn, then you will probably walk away a loser. You must always be prepared to negotiate, and you should expect to earn what you are worth 90 percent of the time. To do this, you need to figure out in advance what the general fee ranges will be for your services.

One independent literary agent discusses the dangers in thinking only of what your time is worth hourly when you work for yourself. He says, "Some agents tell me that they won't spend much time looking over a contract for $7,500 on which they are going to earn only $750 because they figure their time is worth X amount per hour, and they simply cannot afford to do this. I take the opposite view. Of course, I always prefer to work on a $20,000 or $50,000 or $100,000 book contract where I may earn $3,000 for one hour's work, but I also figure that since I earn that $3,000 for one hour, then I can afford to earn $20 an hour on another contract. That's where it becomes difficult, if not impossible, to establish an hourly rate for some kinds of freelance work."

A writer who writes under his own name for various publishers and also does a considerable amount of ghostwriting takes a similar view: "I always gain more satisfaction out of my own writing, the stuff to which I attach my name, than I do from the ghosting jobs, but the ghosting jobs pay more. Let's say I earn $150 a page when I ghost. No publisher has yet paid that much per page when I write under my own name. But I figure I use the ghosting to support my own publishing endeavors—which will someday, I hope, pay me more."

Overpricing Versus Underpricing

When setting your fees, take care that you neither under- nor overprice yourself. Both spell disaster. If you underprice, you will always be trying to make ends meet, never earning as much as you could and possibly never earning enough to make a go of freelancing. You are also less valued, most freelancers feel, if you work cheap.

Sharon Neely, who has recently become successful enough to turn down work, thinks setting her rates a little high has been good for her business overall. She notes, "I can afford to charge my new clients more than I charge my old ones because I am turning down business. At first it scared me to turn down business, but I quickly got into the swing of it. Then I saw the connection between that and what I charged. Even as a beginner I resented working for some clients who did not pay well, and my goal always was to weed out those people. My rates have always been somewhat high. My instincts tell me that it impresses the people I work for. They think because they are paying more, they are getting more, the same way that they are more eager to hire me and will call me back right away when I'm too busy to take work. My work is good—I think they are getting more."

Another freelancer reports, "I often raise my rates during recessions. I get more work because publishers tend to fire staff and use freelancers more. It's cheaper for them. When money is tight for a client, though, it is tight for me, so that's when I ask for higher rates. Inflation hits everyone."

If underpricing won't let you earn a healthy living, neither will over-pricing, which may be an even greater danger in freelancing since no one may tell you this is the reason you aren't getting any work. If you overprice, you lose work to persons as qualified or even less quali-fied than you are who charge less. You also won't get repeat business.

CALCULATING YOUR FEES

Figuring out what to charge, not only when you are just starting out but also when you have been freelancing for a few years, is tough but not impossible. Large companies typically use a formula to set prices. They factor in the cost of making a product (something most free-lancers do not have), as well as overhead and profit, and then they use these figures to set a price. While freelancers must also take ac-count of such things as overhead and the cost of producing a service, setting a price is rarely so straightforward a process for a freelancer as it is for other businesses. For one thing, if you work out of your home, your overhead may be so minimal as to hardly be worth cal-culating. For another, your profits may be enormous—200 or even 300 percent compared to 4 to 5 percent for a major corporation—while your hourly earnings may hover at subsistence level.

To figure out what you should charge, begin by calculating your direct labor costs, that is, the expenses related to the preparation of your service. It is easier to calculate if you produce a product or use supplies to prepare or provide your service. The expense of prepar-ing a service can also be irrelevant in certain freelance businesses. An editor working on a manuscript, for example, may find that she uses two pencils and three sheets of paper, a negligible amount of supplies for purposes of determining what she should charge.

Another component of cost is overhead, that is, the amount spent on rent, utilities, support staff, and supplies like paper and pencils that are not directly related to the creation of a service or product.

The last component of cost is the number of hours you spend on a project, also known as the direct labor cost. This is the trickiest figure for a new freelancer to arrive at, and estimating labor costs is difficult even for longtime freelancers.

Clients sometimes help out by suggesting how much time they think a project will take, but these estimates are usually on the low side because the client wants to pay you as little as possible. Another tactic is to confer with colleagues about the time required to do a job and the fee they would charge for doing it, but competitors may not be willing to discuss this, or they may inflate their prices to make themselves look even more successful than they are. Once you have figures from both sources, though, you can often make a pretty good judgment of what you can reasonably charge.

Overhead and the cost of labor (your hourly fee) together are the cost of providing your service. Once you have determined this, the next step is to determine what your profit should be. This is the stage that freelancers like to omit. But every business needs to earn a profit. Profit carries you through the bad times and the good ones. In bad times, it is your cushion. In good ones, it is the money to use for expansion. It is, to put it in concrete terms, how you move to a bigger office or buy a better computer. And after the twin goals of savings and expansion are met, profit always can be distributed as a bonus. After all, that's what the big guys do with excess profits.

The amount of profit that any business earns is highly variable, but most businesses have a natural profit range. As you begin to play with the figures, you will see what your profit range is. And you will find it hard to exceed it by very much.

The bottom line is that you need to show a profit to be successful, even to stay in business. If what you have left after subtracting cost and direct labor is a reasonable profit, then it is enough. If there is too little profit to fund expansion or carry you through a recession, then you need to charge more or provide a cheaper service. Most freelancers, being service businesses, find it difficult to provide a cheaper service, but many do undercharge for their services, especially when starting out, so massaging figures such as your overhead and labor costs is a good way to determine whether you have boosted profits as much as you can. One thing occasionally skews a freelancer's profit picture: Freelancers can show unusually large profits percentages that have little to do with their actual earnings. An editor who works out of her home, for example, shows a profit of 100 percent over her costs on an hourly fee of $50. Art dealers in big cities routinely achieve a profit of 400 to 500 percent, but their earnings do not always match. Because these profits are skewed, you are better off measuring profit in actual dollars rather than in percentages, or in both.

Another approach to profit is through the back door, so to speak. Instead of calculating your cost and direct labor and then playing around with various profit figures, plug in the annual earnings of colleagues and assume for now that this is what you will earn. Then subtract overhead and hourly fees. What is left is profit. Ask yourself if it is enough. Of course, once you are actually operating your business, you will find yourself constantly fine-tuning your fees in order to earn more profit.

Once you have arrived at the cost of providing your service plus a reasonable amount of profit (or an outrageous amount if you can manage it), you are ready to set your prices. Price is the cost of providing your service plus the profit. It is what you charge your customers.

NEGOTIATING FEES

Once you have determined how much you must charge for your services, the next step is to negotiate that amount, or something close to it, with clients.

To negotiate well, you need a lot of self-confidence. You have to appreciate what your services are worth (a lot!) and be able to convince someone else of that. What you do not have to do that scares many people is think quickly on your feet. When most freelancers think of negotiating, they often picture the tough corporate executive who always knows instantly what is the right thing to do. That, fortunately, is not what negotiating is all about—or at least the level of negotiating that freelancers do. In freelance negotiating, you not only can, but you must, use your own personal style. And usually, perseverance goes a lot further than toughness.

If you have done your homework and considered your fee carefully before setting it, then most of the time the fee you ask for eventually will be accepted. When someone does decide to negotiate with you, these negotiations will be based on your initial asking price. Set your fee fairly high when you think you will have to negotiate, but keep it at market value, taking your experience and the going rate into account. Consider, for example, the difference in negotiations when you ask for $30 and when you ask for $50. If $30 is over budget, the client may try to reduce your fee to $20. He would never attempt to reduce it to $20, on the other hand, if your asking price had been $50 per hour. It may come down to $40 or $45, which is still double the $20 fee.

If possible, let the person with whom you are negotiating name a figure first. You can always negotiate upward from there, but once you have named a lower figure, you can never recoup the loss. One reason never to name your fee first is the Gulp Factor. You want the client to gulp when he hears how much you expect to earn. If he accepts your price readily, without a gulp, you can assume that you have charged too little.

If you can help it, never be forced into getting an estimate or naming a price, especially for a big job, right off the top of your head.

Always insist that you need time to think this over. Ask to see some of the work you will be doing or a proposal of what will be expected of you. In almost every field, there is something you can see that will help you size up what the work is worth. Wherever possible, be sure to get your hands on this, whether it is part of a manuscript to be edited, an outline for a book, a musical score that needs a lyricist, an unproduced play that needs a director, or a play that needs a set.

Do stay open to the give-and-take of negotiating. Sometimes you can trade off a reduced fee for something else. For example, if you ask for $3,000 and settle for $2,000, that may not be unreasonable if more work is forthcoming. If this happens, explain that you will lower this fee one time, on the condition that if the client likes your work, he will be willing to pay your full fee the next time. Usually, he will. Or if there are two projects, you might lower your fee if you are assigned both at the same time—in writing.

Finally, although this may seem minor, when you are going to negotiate fees with someone you do not know, dress well. People form instant impressions. And if you walk into a negotiating session in messy or inappropriate clothes, the other person will immediately take your measure—and possibly decide that money does not matter to you. If you are sized up as someone who does not expect very much, not very much is exactly what you will get.

Here are some additional hints on negotiating freelance fees:

- Don't accept the first offer. If you ask for $50 and are offered $40, quickly come back with $45.
- Don't use personal needs as a reason why you should be paid a certain fee. No one cares if you have alimony to pay or need a more expensive apartment.
- Be aware of your worth; you may have to defend it (more on that later).
- Concentrate on selling your strengths, not your weaknesses. That makes you worth more. Never talk about what you can't do or haven't done. Either say you're sure you could learn something quickly or that while you cannot do *A*, you are very good at doing *B*.
- Don't talk money until you are sure the person wants to hire you. Before someone knows she wants you to work for her, a high fee could make you look less desirable. After someone definitely wants to hire you, she will be eager to work out something amenable to you both. This is even more true for freelance employees than for full-time ones. A company that has a pay scale and simply cannot hire you at a certain price may pay you more than that to work freelance, which brings us to a touchy point: defending your worth.

Occasionally, someone may be crass enough to point out to you that your freelance fee is higher than the salary paid to a full-time employee who does the same kind of work you do. Your response should be, "That's true, but the total cost of getting the work done is less. You don't have to provide me with benefits, vacations, Social Security, and you don't have to pay a bookkeeper to keep track of all that."

You also may find that the announcement of your fee is greeted with something like, "But that is more than we usually pay freelancers." There are two possible responses to this: "I'm worth it," and "Then start me low and give a raise on the next assignment if you like my work." If that doesn't close out the conversation, you might add, "This job is a lot of responsibility and work, and I want the pay to be commensurate."

Once the fee has been set, be sure to jot it down somewhere. Illusions of glory in the heady aftermath of successful negotiations have been known to strike freelancers and cause them to remember fees as being slightly or even greatly higher than they actually were.

The Question of Overtime

Freelancers rarely can charge overtime for their work since they do the work entirely on their own time. If you choose not to work from 9 A.M. to 5 P.M. when the rest of the world works and want to charge extra for working 5 P.M. to 2 A.M., you will not have a chance. Alternately, if you claim that you will have to work long or excessive hours on a project, it is not likely to carry much weight with a client, who will probably pull part of the project and give it to someone else.

There is one time, however, when you can justify charging overtime, and that is when a client calls you for a rush job or to work over a weekend or on a holiday. If a client wants a job done too quickly for your taste but in a reasonable amount of time, charging overtime will not work, but if a client wants a job done in a very big and unreasonable rush, in such a way that you clearly would have to work overtime on evenings and weekends, then you can charge extra. Alternately, you can raise your hourly rate or add a percentage surcharge, whichever you and the client agree to. If the client is truly in need of your services, this is one time when he will probably gladly pay overtime charges.

Charging Expenses to Clients

Freelancers must also decide whether to bill clients for expenses such as messenger services, copying, postage, telephone calls, and similar items.

If you bill the client for miscellaneous expenses and are reimbursed, then you cannot deduct these expenses on your tax return. On the other hand, if expenses run high, and your funds are tight, you may want to bill for expenses.

Freelancers bill expenses in one of two ways: They either add them in a clearly itemized fashion to the invoice they submit, or they bury them in the bill. One freelancer who uses a messenger to pick up work, for example, simply adds an hour or two to the cost of the job. Even freelancers who do their own pickups and deliveries often charge for this service by adding their time to the bill.

Package Prices

A package price, as per-job prices or flat fees are often called, is nothing to worry about if you know how to calculate it. If you don't, it is an excellent way to lose money. First, never quote a package price unless the work is clearly defined and limited. Freelance librarian Bryan Johnson never accepts a package price, for, as he says, "I work hourly because people tend to find still more work for me while I'm working on one project. If I had established a package price, I might get caught."

Sally Chapralis, whose stint as a public-relations freelancer led to many different kinds of assignments, notes, "Unlike straight editing where I could charge an hourly fee, the public-relations work didn't lend itself to that. Even when I work in someone's office at an hourly fee, I often end up doing projects such as newsletters or brochures that I would have charged more for had I been working for an hourly fee. Generally, for a brochure or report or presentation, I offer a package price that includes one rough workup and one final copy of the work; anything beyond that gets billed at an hourly rate." Her method is good for people in public relations, advertising, commercial art, and other areas where the limits of an assignment are difficult to define.

In calculating a package price, figure out exactly how many hours you will spend on a project, add in all your expenses, and then add 10 to 15 percent to be sure you are covered. If you can't project the number of hours that will be needed, follow this suggestion from Sharon Neely: "I edit a few pages until I find my pace on a project. After that, it is easy to know exactly how many hours I will need to complete a project." When you submit a package price—before you do the work—send a letter stating what the fee will be and exactly what it will cover. Note that any additional work will be billed at the regular hourly rate. Clients will have no qualms about asking you to do rewrites or fix something in some other way if you have accepted a package price, so be sure to state exactly how much "fixing" you will do for the project.

No project should include an unlimited amount of repair work, particularly if it results from a client simply changing his mind about what is needed. If you sense that you have a client like this on your hands, decline to work for a package price if you can. Often if a client wants the package price only so he can take advantage of you, he will probably back off from the package price when he realizes that this is not going to be possible.

Sometimes freelancers establish a flat fee that is negotiable if they end up doing more work than was originally intended. A negotiable flat fee is generally bad business practice for a couple of reasons. First, if you set a fee and then decide that you really need to charge more midway through a project, you may end up looking unprofessional—or worse, like a whiner. You should be able to establish a fee at the outset of a project and stick to it. If you cannot do this, do not work for a flat fee.

Second, although a negotiable flat fee is often based on whether you are asked to do extra work, you and your client may not see eye-to-eye on what comprises extra work. What you consider a major overhaul, she may claim is minor reworking. If there are likely to be gray areas such as this, your best bet is to decline to work for a package price at all.

WORKING ON SPECULATION AND CONSIGNMENT

Especially as a new freelancer, you will occasionally be asked to work on speculation ("spec") or on consignment. When you work on speculation, you write or produce something for no pay and submit it to someone who you hope will buy it. Usually, the potential client has expressed an interest in your work, but there is no firm commitment to buy.

When you work on consignment, in contrast, you place a work with a seller who is basically an intermediary, such as an art gallery owner, and you get paid when—and if—the work sells. Some freelancers— artists, for example—have no choice but to work on consignment, but most other professionals will not work on speculation.

The advantages of working on consignment are as follows:

- Your work is seen by persons who might not see it otherwise.
- You have a greater chance of selling something than if you refuse to work on consignment.
- This may be the only way to get started, especially if you lack contacts or are switching fields.

The argument in favor of working on consignment can be summarized by saying that you have nothing to lose. If you have no choice but to work this way, then by all means go ahead. You cannot buck the trade custom and will only cut yourself off from important sources of income.

But for freelance writers and others in similar fields who are often asked to work on spec, it is better by far to avoid this if at all possible. Consider these disadvantages to both spec and consignment work:

- You get no money until your work produces sales, if on consignment, or until the work is accepted, if on spec. When you work on spec, the buyer is essentially under no pressure to buy your work.
- The money you spend on an assignment is tied up until you sell

the work—and then, the money may be slow coming in. Work sold on consignment often does not reap any financial rewards until months after the sale; persons who work on spec often are not paid very quickly, either. Freelancers, unfortunately, often are at the bottom of a long list of suppliers to be paid, but this is especially true with spec work and work done on consignment.

• It is not professional. One writer has worked out an excellent response to anyone who asks her to write on spec, as new clients occasionally do despite her experience. She always says, very sweetly, "I would love to do that, but I write for a living, so I can't afford to do any spec work."

Fortunately, the offer to work on spec may only be a bluff. One writer with impeccable credentials but new to a particular magazine was told that they hired new writers only on spec. She offered her regrets and said she never worked that way. The editor and writer parted company amicably, and about four hours later the same editor who could hire new writers only on spec called back with a fat, firm assignment.

Another writer who had recently switched from public relations to writing articles about beauty was asked to work on spec. At first she was inclined to accept, since the editor's argument that she was switching fields seemed to make sense. She was smart enough to say she would have to think it over since she normally did not write on spec. Unwilling to confront the editor on the phone, she wrote a note saying that she could not work on spec but would do the article for $1,200, which was half her usual fee. The editor accepted her offer as if there had never been any discussion of working on speculation.

Moral: Even if you feel you have no choice but to do some work on spec or consignment, always try to bluff your way out of it first. And as soon as you have enough clout not to work this way, don't. The only way to get out of working on speculation is to say no. The way to lessen the hazards of working on consignment is to ask for a draw or insist on payment within a certain amount of time after a sale is made. Once you have established a reputation, these are not hard things to negotiate.

THE QUESTION OF CREDIT

Most freelancers are too small to be able to extend credit to their customers. Their cash flow is not smooth enough, and they can't afford to give up the time needed to collect on overdue monies. Most freelancers are aware of this, though, and never consciously extend credit to anyone. Surprisingly, though, many do extend credit without realizing it. You do this any time a customer owes you money and doesn't pay you. That customer is getting an interest-free loan from you. In effect, freelancers extend credit by letting bills go too long and by not collecting promptly on overdue bills. Usually, too, when you find yourself in this situation, you are likely to have a deadbeat on your hands, which means that you must take immediate action.

You should always have a deadline for when you consider a bill overdue, and when that deadline arrives, you should do something to get your money. One of the ground rules of freelancing is that the person who makes the biggest fuss is often the one who gets paid the fastest.

One freelance commercial artist reports this story about his first job, which was for a major airline. He knew they were good for the money, and he was surprised when it didn't arrive promptly. After thirty days—his limit for payment of a bill—he went to the airline's central office and started complaining. Since the airline was a huge corporation, people were surprised at his personal touch, and while eager to pay him, no one seemed to know quite how to go about getting him his money. He bounced from manager to manager, carried forms, showed copies of his invoice, until he finally got a check that was specially drawn for him—all after being told that this was impossible. He also never had to go through that again, primarily because the airline knows he will become a pest if not paid promptly. And yes, he continues to work for the airline.

Dunning on Overdue Bills

The minute a bill is overdue—whether you decide that is after ten, twenty, or thirty days is up to you—print out a second invoice. In capital letters, type SECOND INVOICE on it. (Most financial-management or accounting software programs can be programmed to remind you of overdue bills.)

The next step is to call the person who hired you to remind him or her that you have not been paid. Sometimes you can do this under the guise of checking to see how he or she liked your work, and just incidentally mention that you haven't been paid yet. If your client shows dismay and promises to attend to the situation, you probably will be paid right away.

Different freelancers use different techniques at the next stage of bill collection. If you haven't heard anything within ten or fifteen days, then you must do something else. One sure way not to be paid on time is to get a reputation as someone who never follows up on such matters. This is one time when being a pest works in your favor. One freelance editor reports, "I keep bugging the editor who hired me. I figure it is her responsibility to nag accounting until I'm paid."

Another freelancer says, "I immediately go over the client's head to accounting. Nine times out of ten the client never even knows I've called accounting. I'm very nice—say I'm just checking on my bill. I always get the name of the person in accounting, and I make sure he or she knows my name. I never let the person call me back; I always insist on calling back myself. This usually works, and I get paid right away. And after I've tracked down my money this way several times, the people in accounting catch on, and I get paid promptly." She adds, "There's another advantage to going directly to accounting, aside from the fact that they get to know you, and that is that you often learn when checks are issued. For example, if you submitted an invoice the last week in a month, and you know the company pays on the first and the fifteenth, then you know enough to call right after the fifteenth if you haven't been paid."

Another freelancer who goes directly to accounting warns, "You can usually do this only with large companies. I often work for individuals who own the company. I would never go over—or rather, under—this person's head to the accounting department."

If your second invoice and several phone calls are ignored, it is time to write an official letter, one that reiterates what has happened, states the amount you are owed, and indicates that this is the last formal warning. It is not worth your time to hire a lawyer to do this, but if you have a good friend who happens to be a lawyer, then his or her letterhead might carry more weight than yours.

There are, of course, some ways to entice your client into paying before the bill is overdue. One is to consider charging interest on bills not paid promptly. To do this add a statement to your invoice indicating that you will charge interest if the bill is not paid in a certain number of days. Then on the second invoice, add the interest charges.

Of course, it is possible to do this only in fields where this practice is generally accepted. The fashion industry and commercial arts generally follow this practice, but anyone working in publishing—where pay is notoriously late—would be laughed out the door for even suggesting that anyone pay interest on an overdue bill. A more positive option, again available only if your industry accepts it, is to offer a discount for early payment. This works for many freelancers.

Once a bill is severely overdue, you must follow up on it in person. When you call someone about an overdue bill, don't hesitate to trade on being a small business, as freelance organizer Stephanie Winston did with a major New York corporation that did not pay her promptly. She said, "I called a vice president and said, 'Listen, I'm a small vendor,' and then I got my check right away. I allow about thirty days before I start agitating. I call the person who hired me when I send a second invoice."

Always maintain close contact with anyone who owes you money. Silence from you may cause your creditor to think you have gone away or given up. On the other hand, don't make any threats that you do not intend to carry through.

Once an account is seriously in arrears and after you have sent at least one invoice and a letter, you can do one of two things: (1) turn the matter over to a lawyer, or (2) file in small-claims court. Either gesture often has a magic touch. One freelancer told of a client who arbitrarily refused to pay because the project had been canceled, something, she noted, "that did not change the fact that I had done my work on the project and expected to be paid. I said I would sue, and I did. We settled out of court for about half of the bill."

Here's a tip: The first time you get paid—especially by an individual or itty-bitty company—make a note (on back of Rolodex cards) of the bank and account number. If you ever need to attach his or her checking account for nonpayment, you'll need this information.

Few freelancers have to sue, and those who do often settle out of court. Since you don't want to run up a large legal bill, it may be a better use of your time and money to try to settle out of court.

Almost every state has a small-claims court where you can file for a small fee, describe your case to a judge or other arbiter, and get an immediate decision. You need not take a lawyer into small-claims court, and the person you sue cannot take one to court either. There are monetary limits in most small-claims courts; they range from several hundred to several thousand dollars, depending on the state.

If you have a legal problem and little money, it is worthwhile to try to find free or inexpensive legal services. Free legal counseling is offered by some professional groups. If your legal problem is minor, consider using a legal clinic or storefront legal service even though the lawyer you see may not specialize in your specific field. If your problem is more complicated, or a lot of money is at stake, you should seek the advice of the best legal specialist you can afford, even if you can afford only one meeting with him or her.

Once you are paid, note this in writing, or you may feel the acute embarrassment of one freelancer who called to complain about a bill that had actually been paid: "I consulted for a company, so they paid me a monthly fee. They were a little sleazy, though, and that combined with my overeagerness to be paid meant that I called them one day in my toughest voice and asked where my check was. I had received it a week earlier and simply hadn't carefully noted what month it was for."

Before cashing a check, always examine it carefully. Is it made out to you? Is it for the right amount? Even more important, look for any kind of disclaimer or waiver of your rights. More than one writer has blithely cashed a check only to discover later that by endorsing it he had sold all rights to his work. Another trick is for a past-due creditor to pay you a partial sum, which the two of you may have agreed to, and then mark "paid in full" on the check.

The majority of freelancers cannot report a single incident of not having been paid, but all can report times when they had to go right down to the wire to get their money. One freelancer says, "I've had one stiffed bill. Eventually, I was told by the client that he was going to cut down the bill. Someone later told me that this particular company does that when it has budget problems. I also worked directly with someone I didn't like who didn't like me. The production editor accused me of not getting clearance on one quote. She said she had put in three days on it. I asked what she found out, and she admitted she learned the quote was in the public domain. I said that's why I hadn't cleared it. I suggested that, in the future, she always call me first if she has a question. It went on and on, exchanging letters. After seven months, I said very simply, 'Pay me or I'll see you in court.' They paid me."

When You Suspect Your Client May Not Be Able to Pay

Occasionally, you will have a client whom you do not totally trust to pay for one reason or another. He may personally be upright but work for a company that operates on a shoestring. Or he may be about to go out of business. Sorry businesspeople usually develop a sixth sense for whether someone will be good for the money, but even the best of us can get caught.

What, if anything, can you do to increase your chances of timely payment when you suspect someone is a deadbeat? Many freelancers ask for an advance from such a person. When Barbara Zimmerman does copyright searches for individuals, as opposed to publishers, she always asks for an advance. She notes, "The one time when I forgot to do it, she didn't pay me."

In addition to getting an advance, you can ask to be paid as you turn in segments of work or complete certain aspects of the project.

If you suspect that someone will not be able to pay, take care to put all arrangements in writing. If possible, write something in the letter of agreement or contract that protects your rights should you not be paid. Ghostwriters, for example, often include a clause in a letter of agreement stating that the work belongs to them until they are paid.

RAISING YOUR FEES

On a more cheerful note than nonpayers, consider that the day will come when you will need to or want to raise your fees. Most free-lancers do this sooner or later, although many do it rather casually. A copy editor says, "I do not raise rates regularly, but rather, I have a sliding scale, which I adjust to the status of the client. I also adjust to the difficulty of the assignment. I try to keep a feel for what the market is paying and keep my rates competitive with that."

Zimmerman says, "I raise rates in two ways. First, I just raise them. Then I have rush and nonrush rates. Rush rates apply when I do work quickly or work on weekends. I quote the higher rate to new clients. I generally raise the clients I think will be amenable, and when I have raised most of those, then I raise the ones I may lose. One huge client with a once-a-year project said over lunch, 'No rate raises.' I'm going to have to deal with that, but I'm waiting until I'm in a better position to negotiate that one. They're a large portion of my business, so I'm not raising them now."

Masseuse Robyn Cones has yet another method: "I usually raise a few people who are new. Then I give two months' notice to my regular clients. So far, I've never lost anyone, and my rates have almost doubled since I started. If someone has sent me a lot of business, I will give a free massage. Most people are willing to pay more, which always amazes me, but then I'm still inexpensive compared to what other masseuses charge."

The following guidelines may help you through the sometimes tricky task of raising your rates:

- Tell new clients first.
- Raise old clients only after you have developed new clients at the new rate.

- Be as tactful as possible when you raise rates. You should never apologize, but you can sound contrite and rather sad that you have to do this.
- Be prepared to lose some clients.

Finally, do review your rates regularly. Other workers get raises, and there is no reason that freelancers should be denied this reward for work well done.

11

PUTTING IT IN WRITING

TWO VERY GOOD FRIENDS—AND FREELANCE COLLEAGUES in the writing business—were having a festive lunch to celebrate having decided to work together on a project that neither one had time to handle full time. Julie and Sarah were going to write a newsletter for a corporate client. Julie, who sold the newsletter, would serve as primary liaison with the client, while Sarah would do the bulk of the research. Then each woman would alternate taking charge of the bimonthly publication.

If all went well, they had dreams of expansion; there was even the lucrative possibility of a newsletter they would write and own themselves. That, they both felt, was where the real money was; meanwhile, this was an excellent way to test the waters, both in terms of their ability to work together and in terms of finding out whether they liked writing newsletters.

Only one sour note marred the happy occasion, and that was when Julie pulled out a three-page letter of agreement outlining their shared and separate responsibilities and the financial split. She handed it to her partner, adding, somewhat apologetically, "Look, if you were my mother, I would still insist that we draw up a letter of agreement, so here is one for you to look over. I think of this as a way of protecting not only our business relationship but also our friendship."

Sarah balked, saying that she could not understand why a written agreement was necessary among friends. Eventually, though, both women signed, and they have, despite occasional differences, enjoyed a long, mostly harmonious—and certainly clear-cut—relationship, personally and professionally. Not only does this fable have a happy ending—not always the case in fables—but it has a moral that all freelancers should heed: Put everything you possibly can in writing and be suspicious of anyone who does not want to commit himself or herself to signing an agreement.

In the case of Julie and Sarah, reluctance to sign the letter of agreement genuinely was based on a common but misplaced fear that arrangements that are too businesslike might ruin a friendship. Actually, as any freelancer, or for that matter, any businessperson who has ever worked with friends or acquaintances can report, the opposite is true. Keeping everything as businesslike as possible strengthens the bonds of friendship, not vice versa.

Of course, arguments do arise, but these arguments would come up sooner or later anyway. They are more readily settled if there is something in writing that defines the relationship. If the arrangements are clear-cut from the beginning and in writing, there is a lot less to quarrel about.

When someone who is not your friend shows reluctance to put your agreements in writing, be leery. Ask yourself why. Does this person anticipate that he will not be able to make good on his part of the arrangement, and is he or she looking for a possible way out should this be the case? At the very minimum, you must consider that this person may be trying to cheat you in some way. Occasionally, someone resists putting something in writing because that just isn't the way she does things, or because that isn't the way things are done in your field.

This is still no reason for you not to put your agreements in writing. Brace yourself, forge right ahead, and weather the laughter or derision or whatever you are subjected to for being so businesslike.

Continue to insist on a written agreement. The fact that so much of what freelancers do is casual or handled by spoken agreements is all the more reason to make every possible attempt to firm things up as much as you can.

Putting things in writing does not necessarily mean that every agreement must be presented as formal document. Casual freelance agreements, such as when a copy editor is assigned a manuscript by a managing editor, do not call for either a contract or a formal letter of agreement. A simple confirming note will do, indicating your acceptance of the assignment and the date the work is due, as well as the money you will be owed. The following is an example of a friendly confirming letter:

> Dear Jack:
>
> This is just a note to let you know that I received the manuscript today and will begin work on it first thing tomorrow morning. I'll have it back to you on the twentieth, in return for which I shall submit a bill for $40 per hour for my work. I've edited a few pages, and I think that your estimation that no more than seventy hours will be required is accurate, as usual.
>
> Perhaps we can have lunch when I turn in the work. I'll talk to you, in any event, as work progresses.
>
> Cordially,
> Marie

As you can see, legal language is not called for; first names even suffice. What matters here and in any "official" correspondence you write as a freelancer is that the relevant "facts" or conditions of the agreement are noted in writing.

CREATING A PAPER TRAIL

Invoices, letters of agreement, and contracts are the usual and most common written documents that freelancers use. Most of these, plus your letterhead, can be generated with your computer.

INVOICES

An invoice begins the payment process. Always keep copies of invoices, on paper or on a disk, so you have a quick reference of what you are owed and the date you billed the job. An invoice should include the following information:

1. The date
2. Your name and address
3. Your social security number
4. The name and address of the person for whom you worked
5. Description of the project and number of hours worked
6. Statement telling whether invoice is for full or partial payment
7. Amount of money you are owed
8. Terms, or when due, plus any discounts for early payment or announcement of your intention to charge interest

Some invoices in which various types of billing are shown appear on pages 187–189.

Submitting the Invoice

Depending on the kind of work they do, freelancers have a variety of ways of submitting invoices. Most people submit their bills with the finished project, although if the project is long, they bill monthly or at several points throughout the project. One freelancer notes, "I always send an invoice because it is more professional. Occasionally, a client gives me an invoice form to fill out, and I will do that. Mostly, though, I prefer to submit invoices on my letterhead. I also mail them a day or two after I complete a project. That way, when I have worked on several projects during the month, I can do my billing all at once." Bryan Johnson gives his short-term private library clients an invoice as he leaves a job.

Stephanie Winston, who organizes for private and corporate clients, says, "I walk up to my clients at the end of a day and hand

INVOICE

May 1, 1996

TO: Henry Smith
45 East Fourth Street
New York, New York 10009

FROM: Jane Jackson
1300 Michigan Avenue
Chicago, Illinois 60600
123-45-6789

Family Therapy
20 hours consulting @ $40 per hour $800

NOTE: 10 percent discount for payment remitted within ten days.

them a bill with a smile. They always pay me right then. Corporate clients are different; I submit invoices to them and get paid later."

Never let anyone else prepare an invoice if you can help it. One inexperienced freelancer forgot to write an invoice when he turned over an assignment. The client pressured him for one and offered to type it up on the spot, which the freelancer allowed. Later, when the check arrived in the mail, it was less than the freelancer thought he was owed. When he called the client, he learned that accounting had caught a discrepancy between the total amount and the hours worked. The client had to take the invoice to his boss a second time for approval. By the time the freelancer called, the invoice had been

---

Jane Smith
123½ West 98th Street
New York, New York 10025
987-65-4321

INVOICE

May 1, 1996

TO: John Doe, Publishers, Inc.
20 Oak Street
Chicago, Illinois 60611

Editing and rewriting chapters 1, 3, 5, 6, and 8 of
Family Therapy ms.
60 hours at $25 per hour (partial bill) $1,500

Thank you. Please remit within twenty days.

---

on the boss's desk twice. The client was unwilling to take the invoice to his boss a third time, so while both agreed the money was owed to the freelancer, who had, in fact, not given the correct number of hours to match the total charged, the client suggested that the freelancer make up the loss on the next assignment.

The freelancer felt trapped. The money would obviously be forthcoming, but not for several weeks. Of course, if the freelancer made a fuss, he would have gotten the money sooner, but doing so might have jeopardized his chances of getting that next assignment. Besides, both the client and the freelancer were at fault in this situation. And a

---

INVOICE

DATE: May 1, 1996

TO: John Doe, Producer
Downtown East Theater
45 E. Fourth Street
New York, New York 10009

FROM: Jane Smith
123½ West 98th Street
New York, New York 10025
987-65-4321

Set design of *Doing It Right*

(preliminary sketches, model set,
supervision of building of set) $3,000

---

somewhat sticky situation that, in effect, did cost the freelancer money, could have been avoided had the freelancer written his own invoice.

Most freelancers like the idea of breaking up a large bill, if only for psychological reasons. One person notes, "I bill midway through a project and at the end. For a big project I bill four or five times. I found out that the size of the bills boggled people's minds, and they handled smaller bills more easily. Billing a big job each month also helps my cash flow."

Another astute freelancer comments, "I also pay attention to the round figures on an invoice. If my hourly rate works out to a total of $4,000, I may decide to bill $3,800 because it looks like much less than $4,000.

LETTERS OF AGREEMENT

Letters of agreement can be used whenever you are working on a long-term project or a project so complicated that it requires a contract of some sort. In fact, letters of agreement are contracts, although they are often—but not always—written in less formal language. Whenever possible, try to be the person who writes a letter of agreement. You will still negotiate its terms, but you will have an advantage in having produced the first terms of the agreement.

One freelancer describes her system for writing letters: "I never feel more businesslike than when I am drawing up a letter of agreement. First, I go through my old file of letters of agreement to see if there is one I can modify to this situation. I always keep letters of agreement in my computer. The first one I ever wrote was modeled after one my agent had written for me and another writer, and I think I've essentially been revising that one ever since. Then I write out a list of the things I want to cover in this agreement. I put the list aside. When I look at it again, the next day or even a few hours later, I often think of something to add. Finally, I write the letter of agreement. I use first names if the letter is with someone I know well, but I make sure it looks official. I always type in lines where the signatures are to go, for example." (See sample letter of agreement below.)

Informal Letter of Agreement

Another freelancer reports on a method he employs for putting things in writing when he senses resistance to a written form: "I write a confirming letter in which I restate everything we have agreed to verbally—the price, the deadline, the amount of work I will do for the price." A word of warning: Since this kind of letter is not signed by both parties to the agreement, it does not carry the weight of either a letter of agreement or a contract. On the other hand, should questions arise later concerning the nature of the work, the letter still is better than having only a verbal agreement. Several samples of informal confirming letters follow.

LINDBERG-ELMER Letter of Agreement

October 11, 1999

Frances Lindberg   Patricia Elmer
414 West 91st Street   527 West 98th Street
New York, New York 10025   New York, New York 10025

Dear Patricia:

Our signatures at the bottom of this letter of agreement will signify our acceptance of the terms described herein regarding the preparations for the manuscript tentatively titled *Nutrition*, due to be delivered on December 1, 2002, to Fred Jones.

1. Frances will deliver to Patricia all notes and other work pertaining to the manuscript, along with an outline of content of each chapter.

2. Patricia will use these materials to write a manuscript of approximately 75,000 words.

3. Frances will edit Patricia's work, and if rewriting is required, Patricia shall undertake it upon receiving specific, written directions from Frances.

4. Expenses incurred during the preparation of this manuscript, such as copying and typing, shall be shared equally between Frances and Patricia.

5. All monies to be paid for this project shall be rendered by Daniel O'Neill, literary agent, to Frances, less agent's fee, who shall in turn be responsible for rendering the following flat fee to Patricia: $10,000.

6. If Patricia fails to produce a manuscript satisfactory to Frances within the time agreed, Frances may, at her option, terminate this agreement. In the event of such a termination, Patricia shall re-

tain all sums received by her and shall forfeit all further interest in the work, and shall return to Frances all materials related to the book.

ACCEPTED

_____

Patricia Elmer

_____

Frances Lindberg

DATE_____

ALLISON-STROMBERG Contract

January 23, 1996

James Allison   Joe Stromberg
5749 Fairfield   4212 Olive Street
Chicago, Illinois 60659   Elgin, Illinois 60120

Dear Jim:

This letter summarizes the agreement that the two of us have entered as of this date, whereby I shall develop and submit to you a proposal for revising the workload structure of your fabric-manufacturing plant. The terms of the agreement are as follows:

1. You shall instruct your appropriate department heads to open all records to me that relate to the operations of the plant and its workers.

2. I am obligated to work under strictest confidentiality regarding any information I obtain related to the operations of your plant.

3. Within eight weeks I shall submit to you in writing a proposal for plant reorganization. The report shall include details of function as well as of cost.

4. Within three weeks you will review the project and meet with me to discuss those suggestions that are immediately applicable. After

this meeting I shall submit a revised report within three weeks of those suggestions requiring further work.

5. The terms of payment are as follows: $12,100, payable half on signature of this letter, one-fourth on completion of initial report, and one-fourth on completion of final, revised report.

Please sign all copies of this letter. Keep one for your files and return one copy to me for my files.

Accepted and agreed to by:

_____   _____
James Allison   Joe Stromberg

WITNESSED BY: _____

DATE: _____

Here is a checklist of things to include in most letters of agreement, informal or formal:

☐ Complete names and addresses of both parties.
☐ The date of the letter of agreement, which can appear at the top or bottom of the letter or contract.
☐ Description of project, including dates when work is to be turned over and amounts of monies owed.
☐ Who owns the work or services you provide (if applicable to your field). When writers do "work for hire," for example, that work is usually owned by the person who commissions it.
☐ Places for all parties to sign and a line for witnesses, if necessary. A witness is necessary if the letter or contract is liable to be questioned. Anyone can witness the signatures, or you can have a notary witness them. Witnesses, which are very important in wills, for which the primary signatory will not be around to confirm his or her signature, are far less important in the kinds of contracts freelancers draw up.

EXCHANGE: THE ESSENCE OF A CONTRACT

The element of exchange is the essence of any contract or letter of agreement. This means that you give something, and in return you get something back. For most freelancers, this involves giving a service, and getting back, in exchange, payment for the service. This element of exchange must be present in every letter of agreement or contract that you write or are party to.

Apart from the element of exchange, when writing a letter of agreement (or a contract) try to cover every possible contingency: what you are responsible for, what the other party or parties are responsible for, who will owe whom what amount of money, when the money is to be paid, what specific materials or supplies that one party is to supply to another, and what will happen in the event that the project does not work out.

A Special Situation: Letters of Agreement for Work Left on Consignment

Artists and craftspersons are often forced to place their work in galleries on consignment, which means they will be paid when and if the work is sold. Without passing judgment on the fairness of this system, no artist or other freelancer should leave work with someone else without drawing up a letter of agreement. (Amazingly enough, many gallery owners do not routinely do this.) It does not matter who draws up the letter of agreement so long as one is drawn up. It should be in the same format as the letters shown above. The list that follows provides specific guidelines for what should appear in this kind of agreement.

- The exact amount you will be paid if the work is sold/accepted.
- Who has responsibility for loss. When artwork, for example, is placed in a gallery on consignment, it is usually the artist who bears the responsibility if it is lost or damaged, but often you can get a gallery to share this responsibility with you. You should always try to do so.

- The conditions for storage and display. Be very specific here so you will have a case if the artwork is damaged.
- The period of time work can be displayed; if work is done on speculation, then note the period of time during which work must be accepted. After that the assumption is that you may pull your work and show it elsewhere.
- When you will be paid. If a gallery sells your work for a sizable sum but agrees to time payments, is it obligated to pay you when the sale is made, or do you receive your fee in lump sums as the gallery is paid? The letter of agreement or contract should note in fact whether you find it acceptable to have your work paid for over time.

DEALING WITH CONTRACTS

Most freelancers occasionally have to deal with contracts, which are nothing more than detailed letters of agreement. Sometimes a business will change so that where contracts were not normally used, they now will be. Due to changes in the copyright law, this has happened with magazine writers in recent years.

Contracts have a way of looking as if they were written in stone. They are usually prepared by a lawyer, which means they are written in legalese. Your name may even be printed on the contract as if it has always been there.

Don't let this intimidate you. Question anything and everything about a contract that does not suit you. And if the contract is truly complicated, think about asking your own lawyer to take a look at it. Much as you may dislike having to pay legal fees, the amount at stake is a lot more than what you'd pay your lawyer for an hour or two.

Here are a few guidelines to help you deal with contracts:

- Treat every contract like an unfinished document.
- See if the terms of the contract are the terms you agreed to orally. It is a not-unheard-of tactic for a tough (and slightly unscrupu-

lous) negotiator who has agreed to one set of terms orally to change them slightly in the written contract.

- Pay special attention to any areas where you have not yet reached complete agreement. One very tough negotiator once deliberately left some areas of negotiation up in the air when discussing a project. When he prepared a contract, he wrote in exactly what he wanted and hoped the other party would not raise a fuss.
- Check the small details: the spelling of your name, your address.
- Check big points, such as how much you will be paid and how and when payment will be rendered.
- Be sure the contract contains the all-important element of exchange, that is, what you are to deliver and what you are to receive in return.
- If you do not like something in a contract, you may change it, although as a courtesy any proposed changes are usually discussed first. Once you have agreed, simply cross out any offending clause and initial it. The other party will initial the changes as well.
- To add a new clause, type it out and attach the sheet at the appropriate place in the contract. Initial it.
- Keep all copies of contracts. Do not count on anyone else to supply you with a copy, even after all the copies have been signed.

A Moral Fable: Always Read the Small Print— and the Big Print

A writer trusted her agent, with good reason. She trusted him so much that she eventually became quite blasé about signing publishing contracts. One day, she sailed into her agent's office and signed a new contract without even bothering to read it. She then left to celebrate her deal at a restaurant. Not until her copy of the contract arrived a few weeks later did she notice that she had agreed to deliver a three-pound, 120,000-word manuscript in three months rather than three years.

No one, neither the blasé writer nor the agent, had spotted the error in the delivery date. Fortunately all ended well. The publisher laughed when the error was pointed out and agreed to change it.

But what if the publisher had wanted the book earlier, had in fact thought that the book should be delivered sooner rather than later? He would now have had something to negotiate with, because the contract with the three-month deadline was a done deal. The writer would have been in big trouble.

The moral is boring but very important: Read anything and everything, large and small print, before signing it.

12

SETTLING DOWN TO WORK

A MAJOR CHALLENGE TO FREELANCERS—BEGINNERS AND seasoned ones—is how to manage time wisely. Some freelancers worry about working too hard, and freelancing has been known to bring out the workaholic in many people. Others worry that they will lack the discipline required to structure their days. They fear that without a boss or other authority figure looking over their shoulder, they simply won't produce. Ironically, both problems plague all freelancers from time to time; freelancing seems to be the kind of work where you can be a workaholic one month and then feel totally burned out the next. The time and efficiency sacrificed to these problems, however, can be kept to a minimum if you make an effort to manage your time well.

The workaholism may be necessary to get a freelance business off the ground or to ease anxiety over starting a business. It is most often a problem for those who work at home, where the work seems always to be staring you in the face. Most freelancers, though, go through a period of being excessively involved with their work and then taper off. A typical attitude is that of Sharon Neely: "After two years, I'm starting not to work on weekends. I'm feeling more secure and making more money with my editing, so I don't feel the financial need to work weekends." Margaret Stein, also a freelance editor and rewriter, took longer to realize that she need not be such a slave to her business: "For years, especially during my busy season in summer, I worked late practically every night and right through most weekends. I was even earning enough money so I didn't have to do that. It was just my busy season, and I didn't seem to be able to shake the notion that I should kill myself for three or four months out of every year. Finally, I took a summer house out of town. It seems that my concern for money, which had propelled me to work so hard during the summers, now propelled me toward the house every weekend. I couldn't stand not to use the house since I had paid for it. Anyway, it broke the pattern."

As for worries about not having the self-discipline needed to freelance, those who don't simply do not survive very long. Beyond learning how to manage your time, successful freelancing requires a heavy dose of certain personality traits such as discipline, concentration, and the ability to keep the world at bay when necessary.

MANAGING YOUR TIME

When you work for someone, your time is often structured for you. When you work for yourself, you alone are responsible for how you spend your time. There are three things to be concerned with when considering how you spend your working hours: (1) how you actually spend your time, (2) how you should spend it, and (3) how you can improve the ways you spend it.

Setting Your Own Hours

One of the joys of freelancing is the freedom to set your own hours. A few freelancers keep unusual hours, but most settle into a fairly regular work schedule. "Fairly regular hours" usually translate into something resembling the nine-to-five workday, if for no other reason than that is when the rest of the world works. If clients need to

call you, they will do so then. If you need to call them or want to solicit new business, that is when you must do it.

Margaret Stein had a tendency to maintain those hours from the
very beginning, except when she was besieged with work. She recalls,
"The very first day I worked at home, I was very diligent. I had
planned to work long, hard hours. I didn't have on a watch—a sign
of my new freedom that I soon dispensed with—but I felt myself
growing very tired. I guessed it was about seven or seven thirty at
night. I threw down my pencil and decided to give up for the day. To
my surprise, it was five on the nose."

Barbara Zimmerman says, "I try to work nine to five, but I also have
a trade-off. I use the freedom I have to do errands, so I make up for
it by working a little late or on weekends." Many freelancers, such
as Bryan Johnson, rise early to take advantage of the hours of the
morning before the phone starts ringing. He notes, "I often start
work at five or six in the morning, so I can work for about six hours
and then go do something else in the afternoon." Like busy executives, a freelancer soon discovers that even an hour in the morning
before the phone rings can be precious.

If you are going to be a successful freelancer, you should undertake the management of your time seriously. Time-management consultants note that in business, people tend to spend as much as 80
percent of their time on tasks that produce about 20 percent of the
work. Too many people work diligently on low-value activities. These
activities may make them feel very good when completed, but they
aren't real work. Often, office workers, who are basically at the beck
and call of their superiors or at the mercy of the corporation's de-
mands for paperwork, have no choice. As a freelancer, though, you
do have a choice. You will find that with planning and discipline you
can learn to fill the hours of your day with meaningful work—the kind
that brings in a regular paycheck.

One freelancer, when asked how she maintains the self-discipline
to work in her home day after day, year after year, comments, "I
find that what I do during the day is so directly related to how much
food I have on the table that I have no problem getting the work
done."

Time Wasters

The Small Business Administration once published a list of time wasters. Of the external time wasters, the following apply to freelancers:

Telephone calls
Meetings
Visitors
Socializing
Lack of information
Communication breakdown
Excessive paperwork

Of the internal time wasters, these particularly apply to freelancers:

Procrastination
Failure to delegate tasks and responsibilities
Unclear goals
Failure to set priorities
Crisis management
Failure to plan work
Poor scheduling
Trying to do too much in too short a time
Lack of self-discipline
Lack of relevant skills

With some careful thought on how you do handle your time and an ongoing review of your work methods, you can avoid all these pitfalls. Here are some general hints on managing your time:

- Figure out what time of day you are most productive and schedule important work during those hours. Margaret Stein says, "I'm really a morning person, but that is always when the phone rings. I bought myself a phone machine, turned my phone down so I couldn't hear it ring, and I never answer the phone until eleven A.M., at which time I have done about four hours of work."

- Keep a detailed log of how you spend your time. Record your activities for every quarter hour. You will quickly see when and how you waste time, and you will probably be able to spot your most productive hours if you are not aware of them.
- If the log shows a lack of self-discipline, create new time-management habits. Write a fairly rigid schedule for yourself and stick to it until it becomes habit.
- Keep a calendar. All successful executives devise some way of maintaining an accurate calendar, and most live by it. Some maintain a two-calendar system (one for the desk; one for the briefcase), while others rely on a computerized calendar or carry an electronic pocket organizer. Electronic pocket organizers are especially handy devices. In one small handheld instrument, depending on what you spend, you can get a calendar, a notebook, a memo pad, a business/personal/vendors index, a calculator, and lots of other bells and whistles. The best of these can be plugged into your computer, so when the batteries go dead, you need not reenter the information from scratch.

There are also some specific things you can do to manage your time more wisely:

- Bundle similar tasks. For example, do all your telephoning at once or all your letters at one time.
- Relegate the small or routine tasks to your least productive hours. That is when you should write letters (unless it is a very important letter) or make phone calls.
- Get someone else to do work you don't absolutely have to do. Lots of freelancers refuse to consider that they might need office help or an assistant of some kind. But if you are spending too much of your time on routine tasks and too little on your real work, then it is time to think about hiring someone. Get a

student to type letters two hours a week, hire someone to do your routine research on an hourly basis, even think about hiring someone to clean your home (and office) so you don't have to be distracted by that kind of work.

- Use downtime—when you are riding on a bus or waiting for an appointment—to do certain routine or easy tasks, such as figuring your expense account, reviewing a memo for a meeting, looking at the mail, or reading trade journals and magazines.

- Speaking of the mail, resist the urge to do something to it right away. It will always contain something that will make you want to type an immediate response or pick up the phone, but if you have planned to do such routine work later in the day, then stick to your schedule. Toss out junk mail without reading it.

- Control paper. Keep your filing systems simple; always look for ways to streamline.

- Keep things where they belong. This way you will always be able to find them when you need them. And keep them in logical places. If you use a certain file five times a day, it makes no sense to put it in a file drawer after each use. Keep it nearby or on your desk.

- Maintain a good contacts file, one that rests right by your phone or lives in your computer. If you have an electronic pocket organizer, you can also carry your contacts with you. Cross-reference numbers that you use a lot. For example, if you fly to Boston every few weeks, cross-reference all the Boston airlines on one general card and then put specific information such as phone numbers and flight information on separate entry cards.

- Whenever you use a telephone number for the first time, consider whether you should add it to your permanent phone file.

- Put any information that you need while you are on the phone on the main card. If you work with someone whose assistant always answers the phone, note the assistant's name. A phone card should contain not only the phone number but also the complete name, title, and address of the person.

- Use a timer, if necessary, to break up your day into specific tasks, especially if you are trying to train yourself to new work habits.

Making Long-Range Plans

Setting goals and planning your work in advance can help you accomplish more work in the long run. Long-range planning should be done yearly, although you should also keep track of monthly or quarterly earnings for the sake of your cash flow. One freelance writer sets up her schedule on an annual basis: "Every fall I try to set myself up for the rest of the year. I write several short book proposals, knowing that two or three will sell. Beyond that, I usually have a long-term book I'm working on over a period of several years. Then I scout around for one or two major rewriting projects from textbook publishers. That pretty much fills my year. People tell me I'm lucky to be able to set up my year that way, but I work very hard for several weeks to get all that done. And of course, some years things do not fall into place. That can work both ways. One year, I sold too many little books—I was busy every minute."

One freelance design consultant says her financial life was a shambles until she learned to think in terms of yearly planning. She reports, "I have a small regular job as a design consultant; it takes about three days a month and pays $1,000, or $12,000 a year. Then I also am the designer of a small magazine published by a museum; that brings in $10,000 a year. Beyond that base of $22,000, I have learned that I can count on $5,000 to $6,000 in freelance art catalogs a year—they are my real love. I actively look for another $8,000 to $10,000 in miscellaneous design projects—any kind will do—to round out my year."

A freelance financial consultant discusses even more long-range financial planning: "I keep the books for two companies, each of which pays me $15,000 a year. I do this work in their offices, though, and it takes about half my time. Eventually, I want my entire business to be run out of my home and to consist of private clients. Currently, I am picking up another $15,000 in private clients each year. For the last three years, this has escalated by 100 percent. When I started three years ago, I did only $5,000 in private business. My problem is planning when to let one of the companies go since each represents a sizable chunk of income to me. I've decided to hire someone to help me with the private clients so I can increase my volume by more than 100 percent. This way, I figure I can drop one of the companies two years from now and the second company a couple of years later."

Keeping Lists

One way to initiate any planning is to make A, B, and C lists. There are several ways to do this, and you must find the one that suits you. You might draw up an A list of things that are most pressing to get done, a B list for things that are important but can be done over a longer time, and a C list for long-term planning projects.

It always helps to put your ideas in writing. It will make you consider them more seriously. A project that sounds wonderful in your head may not be so great or even possible once you commit it to paper. Here is a way to examine any plan you are considering:

1. Define the problem or describe the project.
2. Describe a possible course of action.
3. Describe the pros and cons of that course of action.
4. Consider the alternatives.
5. Review all possible courses of action.
6. Decide on best course of action.

This list can be used for things as diverse as deciding whether to hire someone to figuring out whether a work project is feasible to deciding whether to invest in new office equipment. It can even be used to structure your day.

Once you have given yourself a red or green light on a project or plan, you need to schedule it—at least as much as you can. Freelancers often find that the nature of their work—which largely consists of waiting for others to give them work—is such that they often cannot schedule projects as well as they'd like to. One freelancer comments, "That's the hard thing about freelance publishing. Nothing runs on schedule. Books are supposed to come, and they don't. I used to set up for projects before they came in, but they rarely came in on schedule. The only way I will block out time now is if I have a written agreement with someone to the effect that I will still be paid even if the work does not come in on time. If I can substitute another project, I do, and then I don't charge the client. If I can't, the client owes me. It gets to be a juggling act, though."

It also helps to know how much time you spend on administrative tasks such as maintaining contact with old clients and soliciting new ones, correspondence, and routine office chores. Keeping a log for a week or two will help you pinpoint how much time is needed for this or any other activity.

THE PRODUCTION SCHEDULE

Offices go round on production schedules, at least well-run ones do. Freelancers often think they can do without them. Nothing could be farther from the truth. Especially if you are juggling more than one project, you need a production schedule that lists the materials you will need, steps that will be required to complete the project, and an estimate of the amount of time you will need to complete each step of the project. The hardest part of any project is calculating the amount of time that you must spend at each step along the way.

There are several ways to determine how much time you will need, and often a combination of these techniques works.

- Ask the client how much time he thinks will be required. You might think that you must take his response with a grain of salt since it will be to his advantage to underestimate the number of hours you will need to work, but in many kinds of freelancing, clients have a realistic and often generous grasp of the number of hours involved in the projects they assigned.

  The key is whether the client has done the kind of work he is asking you to do. If he has, then he probably knows how long it will take. If he hasn't, then he not only doesn't know but you may not even want to give him a chance to mull it over.

- Ask your colleagues how much time they think will be necessary.
- Do a little work on the assignment and project the time you will need based on that.

Even with the very best production schedules, plans often go awry. As a freelancer you will probably never be able to maintain the absolute control you might like over your time and work flow, but you will have your sanity if you at least make some attempt to organize.

An Added Benefit of Advance Planning

There is one other benefit to making short- and long-term plans. In a purely psychological sense and in a very real economic sense, they can help to alleviate some of the insecurity associated with freelancing. If you have scheduled your future projects in writing, you will have a clear idea of when it is time to go after more work and how much work you need to stay solvent.

GETTING ORGANIZED

All freelancers need to be organized. There are, of course, people who work on desks stacked high with paper and projects, but the only people who work successfully in such cluttered surroundings are those who can immediately put their hands on anything they need. If you have to search for something, you are too disorganized. And disorganization has never helped any freelancer become successful. So even if you are the type who is happy surrounded by clutter, make sure it is organized clutter.

Your office should be organized so the things you use regularly are readily accessible. Keep files and reference books near where you work. Also take time to clear out your files regularly. Play around with a filing system until you settle on something that works for you. And be prepared to rethink it occasionally. Too many people make the mistake of setting up an office and viewing it as permanent. Instead, think of your office as a living thing, at least in terms of how you organize it. Rethink your organizational systems occasionally even if it means taking them apart and starting all over.

Learn to control paper flow. Start by doing something with paper right away. If you clip from newspapers and magazines, set up a file to hold the clippings until you find time to sort and file them. When you read your mail, sort it into three stacks: things you must handle right away and things you can handle within a week, and things you need never handle again. The last stack goes directly to the wastebasket.

Keep a notepad near you as you work to jot down things as you think of them. Resist the urge to jump up and do them; just note that they must be done and when.

If your work requires it, get a bulletin board and hang it near your desk. It is an excellent place to display a calendar on which you mark deadlines, as well as production schedules and work-flow charts.

Get in and out baskets if that will help you control the flow of work across your desk. Even these, though, tend to become swollen with papers that are never sorted, so you might want to take a hint from freelance editors who arrange their projects on a shelf or worktable. Don't be afraid to be slightly or even greatly unorthodox as you think about how to organize your desk and office. This isn't a corporation, or if it is, it's your own corporation.

KEEPING THE WORLD AT BAY

Desk organized? Work planned for the next five years? Calendar diligently marked with little and big projects over the next two months? Then the next step is to keep the world at bay so you can get some serious work done. Learning to take the time you need to work is one of the hardest things for a freelancer to do. As Judy Waggoner notes, "There are always the unexpected things that come up: a sick child, a long telephone conversation, other responsibilities such as shopping or chauffeuring."

Freelancers are sitting ducks for friends who have a little extra time on their hands. They know your boss won't pop in the door and give you the evil eye for yakking when you should be working. And in all honesty, since most freelancing is essentially lonely work, freelancers don't exactly flinch when the phone rings, even at the busiest time of day. Despite all this, the day will come when you simply must work without interruption. Or when, if you love your work, you will want to work without interruption. What can you do about it? There are several things.

Control the Phone

First, you must control the telephone. A friend when you are lonely, it is a monster when you are busy. Start by making all your outgoing calls at one time of day. If possible, tell people to call you at a certain time of day. Note: This applies more to friends than clients, but you can even suggest to clients that you are most easily reached at specific hours. Turn on the phone machine and turn off the phone. That way you won't hear the phone ring, and you will get all your messages. If you have an answering service, tell them to pick up on the first ring.

Avoid the Office Time Wasters

People in offices spend an enormous amount of time in meetings and writing reports and memos. Mostly useless time. If you are not careful, you too will spend an enormous amount of time doing the same thing. Clients will always be trying to hook you into their office routines. Either they think you miss it, and they want to include you, or they want you to be as frazzled and unproductive as they are. Either way, don't let it happen to you. To avoid meetings:

- Send your agent.
- Go but announce that you can stay for only a short while. Announce when you have to leave when you arrive or when you schedule the meeting. Not only will this keep the meeting short,

but this kind of time limitation will cut down immensely on the small talk that consumes much of meetings.

- Don't go to a meeting to discuss something you can handle over the phone. And don't handle something over the phone that you can handle in a letter or better yet, by E-mail. If you can work faster over the phone than in writing, then always pick up the phone before resorting to a letter. Of all these methods, E-mail is fastest and most efficient.

Say No

There are three times when you should say no to a client. The first is when you are too busy. You should also say no when you don't know how to do something. It is no use trying to sell talents and skills you don't have. The only result will be that these people will never hire you again. That is a loss you can never recoup in freelancing. Finally, you should say no when someone is taking advantage of you.

By nature many freelancers are quiet, passive people—that is the kind of person who does especially well working alone. To survive in freelancing, you have to throw off enough of your passivity to say no to someone who is not using you well. One freelance editor finally got the nerve to say no to a client who underpaid her when she had developed enough skill to get higher rates from other publishers. A freelance costume designer says she won't work with a producer who doesn't give her enough money to do a project well: "I'm much more likely to quibble over the budget I need to do a job well than my salary. I've let projects fall through over that issue."

FREELANCERS' PITFALLS

There are some pitfalls in freelancing that are not normally encountered in other kinds of work: procrastination and loneliness. Procrastination is especially disastrous. Anyone can procrastinate small-time, but only a freelancer can go to two movies in a row on a

212 SUCCESSFUL FREELANCING

bad day. And people who procrastinate on the boss's time still get paid. Freelancers lose the time and the money.

When You Cannot Work

When you hit a day, or even a few days, when you simple cannot bring yourself to work or when nothing good happens when you try to be productive, the best way to deal with this is directly. Go easy on yourself; it happens to everyone. Acknowledge that you are—at the moment—burned out.

Plan a change of pace. Take an early or a late lunch. Go to two movies, only don't let yourself feel guilty about it. Or do, if it will help when you start work again. Take a walk. Call someone for a chat— preferably someone who works in an office, not a fellow freelancer who will be unable to resist you and thus may also lose valuable work time. If quitting time is near, knock off early.

Fighting yourself on the days when you can't work only causes you to lose more time in the long run. One smart soul comments, "I never used to give myself permission to go do something else when I couldn't get my work done, but then I realized that I wasted the time one way or another anyway. Now, when I see that I really can't work, I take off for an hour or so."

Barbara Lee concurs: "A friend who also freelances asks where it is written that we should work nine to five. Another friend even reminds me that people in offices don't work thirty-five hours every week. And I forget to take into consideration the nights when I work until eight and on weekends."

The Loneliness of the Longtime Freelancer

It would be nice to report that only new freelancers get lonely, bored, or suffer from feelings of isolation. Unfortunately, it is an occupational hazard suffered by practically all freelancers off and on. Even freelancers who deal with people all day suffer from the isolation and occasional boredom. Artists' agent Julie Jensen finds this is true: "I have a lot of contact with people since I call on gallery managers all day and spend several nights each week seeing people professionally. But those aren't friends, with a few exceptions. It's not even a particularly friendly world. There are nights when I just know I have to see or talk to a friend if I'm going to feel at all human." A writer who works long hours alone comments, "I've trained all my friends never to break dinner dates with me. They know I may not have seen another human face for forty-eight hours. I love my work, I like working alone, but yes, I get lonely and need to be with other people simply because I haven't been for a while."

Lest you give up freelancing before you even start, there are things you can do to fight the freelancers' pitfalls:

- Make sure you get out every day. One freelance commodities broker who starts every day with a careful reading of several newspapers is frequently asked why he doesn't just subscribe, rather than head out in all kinds of weather to buy the papers. He says, "Not often, but sometimes that outing to buy the paper is the only time I get out all day. I wouldn't dream of having my morning papers waiting for me on the stoop."
- Intersperse errands with your work. Remember that one of the joys of freelancing is that you never have to go to the grocery store at 5 P.M. when the lines are long.
- Better yet, intersperse exercise with your work. Home-based work is an open invitation to sedentariness. A regular regimen of exercise will yield enormous benefits. You will be more efficient at work, more balanced, more energetic, and healthier.
- Make friends or find colleagues in the neighborhood so you have someone to call for a quick lunch on the spur of the moment.
- If you live in a city where others do the same kind of work you do, organize a group to meet regularly for lunch. For several years, writers on the Upper West Side of New York (where writers are about as common as the brownstones that line the narrow side streets) met weekly at a local pub to discuss or not discuss their business, but certainly for the company.

- Extend yourself to get to know the local business owners. You may not want to have lunch with your dry cleaner, but a quick conversation with him can take the edge off a lonely day.
- Put a reward system into effect on lonely or nonproductive days. Work several hours, then knock off to go to the movies or for a walk. More often than not, you will find yourself mentally prepared to get back to work.
- Let yourself fantasize about the possibilities of success. How would it feel if you got a project earning twice as much as you've ever earned before? If you became a star on Broadway? If *The New York Times* said you were the foremost costume designer of the decade? If your book started climbing the best-seller list? If you landed a big gallery show? Don't get too carried away with fantasy, though, or you will fantasize yourself right out of a career.
- Change your work routine. Try working in the afternoon and doing administrative work in the morning for a few days, or vice versa. Or sleep late and work later in the day.
- Even though the opposite tactic was suggested earlier, try interspersing several small projects among the large ones just for a change of pace.
- Finally, leave some time for your personal life, for meditation, and for thoughts of your future. Too many successful freelancers keep themselves on rigid schedules and account for every single minute of their workdays. This can be the fastest road to burnout.

Burnout

It happens to teachers, business executives, advertising executives—people who work in high-pressure jobs. It also happens to freelancers, but it scares them more because they often must continue working to meet the monthly bills. So what do you do when loneliness and procrastination turn into burnout?

A freelance writer who experienced his first—and he hoped, his last—bout with burnout shares his thoughts on the subject: "I had just finished a book I'd been working on for four years. I was inert. I had lots of work to do and was afraid I couldn't get any of it done. I didn't have the money to flee the country for a six-week vacation. I knew I had to self-prescribe in this situation. I started by talking about it to my friends, who were amazingly sympathetic. They had all seen it coming on, and they encouraged me to accept it and scale down the amount of work I did over the next few months. Fortunately, I was able to do that. I earned a little less, but I'll have a longer work life as a result."

Another freelancer describes her tactic for fighting burnout: "I don't know if this would work for everyone, but I use strenuous exercise to combat burnout. The combination of more time to myself and a way to burn off my anxiety seems to do the trick for me."

Each person has to develop his or her own solution to burnout—and the solution for freelancers often is based on financial need. If you cannot cut back on work, then consider a part-time job doing something totally different for a few months. That way, you can still carry on some of your freelance work and think over whether it is time for you to do something else. While you are thinking, you will also be rejuvenating. And the day will come when you will be ready to do your serious work again. One good thing about burnout that is rarely pointed out in the books and articles on the subject: It need not be permanent unless you decide to make it so.

13

MARKETING THE
FREELANCE BUSINESS

FREELANCERS, LIKE OTHER BUSINESSPEOPLE, NEED TO MARKET themselves and their businesses. This can be hard to do, however, because any marketing freelancers do usually involves self-promotion—something many of us find painfully difficult. Because of this, some freelancers shy away from any formal marketing while others rush in the opposite direction, mounting full-scale advertising and publicity programs whether they need them or not. In fact, the kind and extent of marketing you do depends on what the competition does and, most important, who your customers are.

Generally the competition is an excellent guide to what you must do. If the competition does something and you do nothing, you are probably hurting yourself in the long run. If they run a modest advertising campaign in the local newspaper, it probably will not help for you to run a much bigger one. Whatever the competition does, though, your customers remain the ultimate arbiter of your advertising program. If you do not reach them, your marketing efforts are wasted.

For freelancers, marketing consists of three activities: personal selling, advertising, and publicity. Personal selling is how you present yourself to clients. In advertising, you buy space and time in magazines, newspapers, and on television or radio, to name just a few of the possible mediums, in order to promote your business. Publicity is free promotion—the interview the local newspaper does with you or a demonstration of your services that you give on a talk show.

CREATING AN IMAGE

Before you can engage in any element of marketing, especially advertising and publicity, your business must have an image. Unlike a corporation, this need not involve a sophisticated logo or an advertorial that runs in *Newsweek* magazine. But it is also not something that will emerge naturally, as many freelancers hope. The strongest image is one you design and control.

It begins with how you present yourself to your clients when you are selling them your services. Most freelancers need an image that is an amalgam of their own and their clients' styles. If you wear only antique clothes and funky hats, for example, this is fine if your clients are comfortable with this image. But if your clients are Fortune 500 companies, at least consider that you will inspire more confidence if your dress at least approximates what their employees wear to work.

Savvy freelancers accept that they must sometimes adjust their images to suit their clients. We all like to think that we do not judge people by their appearances, but in fact we do, and appearances are rarely more important than when we are using them to cultivate business. Most freelancers wear jeans to work, but most also have a suit or two hanging in their closets left over from when they worked in an office. It is up to you to decide how far to take the personal image you create, but it is worth giving some thought—before you leave home. Unlike your American Express card, you can't leave home without your image. It goes where you go.

A business's other image is the one that shows up on stationery, calling cards, the sign on your studio, and in any and all advertising or publicity. The good news is that you do not need to invest in fancy logos, four-color calling cards, or highly designed stationery. An overdesigned image could even be off-putting in some businesses.

Freelance businesses are by nature small; therefore it behooves us not to try to project a big-guy image. Stationery that is too elaborate or a too fancily engraved business card is more likely to put off clients than to make them want to hire us.

Because you are small, your image also should not be cute or cloying. Nor can it be out of keeping with the services you provide. A former student insisted on using a logo that consisted of a cartoon figure. This might have been okay had she been a cartoonist or illustrator, but she was a computer expert, so her image undermined her authority.

Your image must match your market niche as well. If yours is a high-end business, then your image will be appropriately high-toned. If yours is a bare-bones kind of business, then image should be simple.

Many freelancers find they do not need a logo, but all require a well-designed business card and stationery. A big question at this stage of planning your image is whether and what kind of title to use. You can use one, but do not make the mistake of papering your business card, stationery, and even advertising with too many titles and credits. Billing yourself as president when in fact you are the only employee can look ostentatious.

On the other hand, sometimes inflation is called for. A title may matter, for example, when you are consulting for corporations. They tend to respond to official-looking stationery, and they are very title-conscious. In this situation, you may find it effective to create an image of a bigger business than actually exists.

A business's image is perhaps its most important selling tool. It literally is the face you present to the world. Therefore it is in your best interest to give considerable thought to what goes into your image.

Marketing: How Much Is Enough?

When planning a marketing campaign, be realistic about what you can spend—and recognize that you need not spend very much. You are not trying to mold a corporate image; you are trying to get clients to buy your freelance services. If you find yourself planning to buy a half-page color ad in a trade magazine when everyone else who does the kind of work you do buys only small 1 1/2-inch-square black-and-white ads, consider your motives. Are you doing this because it will result in business or because it will make you feel important?

The same thing applies to freelancers who seek newspaper publicity. Will it really get you business, or does it simply feel exciting to go after this kind of notice from others? Undeniably, some freelance businesses are built around a well-placed newspaper story or ad campaign, but is yours one of them?

One publicist, well known in her field of plastics, struck out on her own suddenly when she and her employers reached an impasse and she resigned unexpectedly. Since she knew how to do publicity, she started planning a campaign, but before she could send out the first press release announcing the formation of her own agency, the calls started coming in. Two years later she still thought about running a small publicity campaign for herself but also admitted that she never had the time to prepare it. Two nurses who opened a private storefront practice in a small Appalachian community did not even think about garnering publicity to announce themselves simply because they knew nothing about it. Fortunately for them, they did not need it. When they showed up for work that first Monday morning, twenty patients were waiting for them. So before you place an ad, or, for that matter, go after any kind of publicity, consider how it will help.

Both these businesses, though, will eventually need to think about doing some advertising or publicity in order to keep their images before their current clients and to draw new ones.

Like most business owners, freelancers are subject to two traps when dealing with advertising and publicity. The first is to view these items as extras or worse, as frivolous expenses, and thus to spend nothing on them. The second is to spend whatever it takes to create an advertising program. Advertising is fun, and it's easy to get carried away.

The solution to both problems is to establish an advertising budget and then stick to it. An advertising budget consists of two spending categories: the production money and the media money. The production money is used to design ads, stationery, calling cards. The media money is used to buy time and space in whatever mediums you decide to advertise. Many advertising agencies follow the 80-20 rule of allotting an advertising budget. Eighty percent of the money goes into buying time and space, while 20 percent is used to produce the ads.

PERSONAL SELLING

Personal selling is an important and often overlooked component of marketing. Studies show that print ads are less effective advertising tools than personal communications. Since you are the primary personal communicator in your business (another hat to wear!), it behooves you to know how to sell yourself effectively.

Many people understandably feel uncomfortable doing this, but this does not mean you cannot be good at it. Selling is a skill that can be learned. If you do not know much about it, think about taking a course in personal selling. Read books and magazine articles to pick up additional pointers. Take an assertiveness training course if you feel you need to be more forceful. You can teach yourself to sell—and sell well—and it is a smart thing to learn when you freelance.

Another reason to work on your sales skills is that freelancers are always selling, even when they think they are off-duty. Wherever people congregate, the topic of work usually comes up, and freelancers are a subject of great interest to others. As you explain your business to others, you are more often than not, even unwittingly, making a sales pitch.

PLANNING AN ADVERTISING PROGRAM

The best advertising programs are planned ones. Too many people get carried away with the glamour of advertising and spend far too much time and money on it. The following steps will help you design an advertising program that is under control.

1. Establish a budget. Decide how much—or how little—you can spend, and stick to it.
2. Investigate the mediums that are open to you—print, direct mail, posters, letters.
3. Establish a goal; that is, figure out exactly what you hope to accomplish by advertising. For freelancers, this often means one of two things: You either want to remind old customers of your services, or you want to find new ones.
4. Carefully plan the timing of your advertising. For an advertising program to be effective, it requires continuity and frequency. Many small-business owners make the mistake of halting all advertising in bad times in order to save money. Or they advertise erratically. Once you decide to advertise, do it steadily. You may advertise less during a recession or a slow period, but you should never stop advertising.

WHERE TO ADVERTISE

Most freelancers do not need to advertise in glossy magazines or on network television. Not only is this too expensive, but it does not reach the target audience of most freelance businesses. Here are some practical, useful places to put your advertising dollar:

- Direct mail. This is far and away the best single source of advertising for a freelance business. Direct mail takes many forms, from a fat, glossy package to a simple postcard, letter, or price list. Direct mail is a sophisticated advertising medium, though, and you would do well to seek expert advice or do some reading on your own before you begin.
- Directories. Often overlooked, directories can be an excellent way to advertise. If they are good, they can really reach your audience and generate new business.
- Trade shows and fairs. If these work for you, there are literally

dozens you can attend throughout the year. Look for the shows and fairs that will draw your target customer.

- Direct display in stores and other outlets. I once saw a clever ad, a small cartoon drawing in a plastic, stand-alone frame. It was promoting an exercise studio, and the owner had placed this unusual display in health food stores and pharmacies near the studio.
- Flyers. Aimed at the right audience, this can be an effective way to advertise.
- Billboards. I'm not talking about the big ones on highways but about the poster-sized displays that show up in buses, subways, and other public places. They are often inexpensive and can work well for certain kinds of small businesses.
- Penny-savers. These small "newspapers" exist to promote local business, and they can be an excellent source of customers. They work well for some businesses, not so well for others.
- Home page. While some on-line marketing is considered publicity and thus is free, there are formats where you pay to advertise. These reach a targeted audience. One effective ad format is a home page. Many freelancers use these interactive devices, which have the great advantage of putting you in touch with customers interested enough to seek you out.
- Specialty advertising. These consist of gifts, large or small, to customers, suppliers, dealers, and the general public who might become customers. The calendar your dry cleaner gives you every New Year is an example of specialty advertising, but this can also take a much more sophisticated form. A gift frequently bears a company's logo, but it need not. A decorator had her logo—a tiny chair—made into a small refrigerator magnet—a great specialty gift that, by the way, did not display her name anywhere. A veterinarian sent his clients door decals designed to inform the fire and police, in the event of an emergency, how many animals were inside the house. His clients, the human ones, that is, loved this gift.

PUBLICITY

Publicity is different from advertising in that you do not pay for it. This can be misleading, though, since it often costs money to prepare publicity. If you are going to give a talk or a demonstration, for example, you may spend money preparing visuals, to say nothing of the time it takes you to prepare yourself. The hours that you spend researching, writing, and rehearsing are direct labor costs. They are time you do not spend producing or delivering your service. If you get carried away with publicity, your earnings could actually drop rather than rise.

As is the case with advertising and personal selling, publicity is a skill that can be acquired. If you do not know much about it, take a course or read books and magazine articles to learn more. The best education about publicity, though, often comes from your colleagues and other freelancers.

Stephanie Winston, who started her business as a personal organizer at a time when no one else had yet thought of doing such a thing professionally, had no choice but to go after publicity. Otherwise no one would know she existed, and people would not understand what she did. Simply running an advertisement describing her personal organizing service was probably not going to work well since she was onto something new—about which the buying public had yet to be informed. Winston acknowledges that she went after the publicity she received by writing press releases that she sent to local New York City newspapers. Her efforts resulted in publicity from *The New York Times*, *The Village Voice*, and *The Wall Street Journal*.

Another woman, who developed a wardrobe consulting service, also focused on publicity as opposed to advertising as her best means of spreading the word about her freelance business. When she started, there were few wardrobe consultants, so she got publicity by capitalizing on that fact. Since then, she has tied her publicity to changing fashion. In spring and fall when the new fashions make an appearance, she sends out press releases announcing that she can help women translate high fashion to practical, business-oriented style. Local radio and television invariably bite, and she has become a staple in both mediums.

One author acts as her own publicist. In the course of doing this, she has learned at least one trick of the trade. Although she writes her own press releases, she signs them with a different name. When television stations and magazines call, she either says that "Jessica Jones" is not there at the moment or she poses as Jessica.

SOURCES OF PUBLICITY

Deciding whether to seek local or national publicity is fairly simple. If your business is local, there is no reason to solicit anything but local publicity. National publicity will not result in sales for you. Good sources of publicity are:

- National or local radio stations. Talk radio is a lively medium that thrives because people are willing to go on air to talk about themselves—and their businesses.
- Local affiliates of network television. Local stations, even those associated with the networks, need local stories. With a little nudging on your part, you could be one.
- Cable television. This is a vast and useful medium, if you can harness it to your needs. Cable television is specialized in two ways that matter to freelancers. One is that locals often host their own shows, usually by buying time, which can be surprisingly inexpensive. These shows are almost always looking for guests. The second means of specialization is by subject matter. Entire networks are devoted to art or history, and fortunately for you, to business. There are also specialized shows that center around, for example, theater or gardening or woodworking. Find the areas that match your specialty, and you are in business.
- On-line. Since you do not pay for "advertisements" and notices sent via the Web, this is strictly speaking publicity. It is a vast,

fruitful, and very useful means of disseminating information. Do
be sure to reach the right audience, that is, one that is local
enough to use your services and in a position to want or need
them.

- Speeches. Never overlook this personal touch. Send press releases to groups and organizations that might be interested in
having you as a speaker.
- In-store demonstrations. Department stores and sometimes
even small specialty stores may be interested in a demonstration if what you sell is tied to what they sell. Use press releases
and personal contacts to get people interested. One of the oldest and most time-honored kinds of "store demonstration," although we often do not think of it in these terms, is an author's
bookstore appearance to sign books.
- Local newspapers and magazines. These are the oldest and most
traditional formats for publicity. Again, regularly spread around
press releases to remind these organizations that you might be
good fodder for a write-up. While major newspapers and magazines will not be right for you, local publications can really work
for you.
- Trade journals. These magazines exist to promote and support
businesses in their field. Virtually every profession has a trade
journal. Find out what yours is if you do not already know, and
then ply it with press releases, most of which they will probably print in one form or another. Also helpful and not too hard
to do is to wangle an article of out a trade publication about your
business. Once you receive this or any other kind of publicity
from a source that does not regularly reach your customers,
copy the story and send it to your mailing list.
- Special events. Open houses, small purposeful parties such as
the ones art galleries often give to open a new show, or studio
demonstrations for a crafts person, all generate business from
new and old clients.
- Bulletin boards. I am not speaking of the computerized version,
but of the local, friendly billboard that lives on a wall near the

door of your pharmacy or grocery store. For certain kinds of businesses, this can be a great source of publicity.

WHEN YOUR MARKETING PLAN WORKS

You will know your marketing plan is working when you begin to receive feedback, usually in the form of new business. One happy freelancer, the recipient of publicity generated by her local newspaper, answered her telephone one morning at 9 A.M. and did not stop answering it until 9 P.M. that evening. She received more than one hundred phone calls and had more business than she could handle if only ten of the calls turned into actual business. This is the payoff, but there is nothing magical about it. This freelancer planned how to market her services, did it, and then sat back to reap the rewards.

14

ENDGAME: EXPAND OR EXIT

SOONER OR LATER, ALL FREELANCE BUSINESSES—ALL businesses, in fact—must either expand or expire. The business that can survive without expansion is very rare, and after a few years of not expanding, most businesses die of attrition.

Some businesses naturally have a limited life span that cannot be controlled, and this forces you either to get out or grow. A freelancer who worked as a manuscript typist even fifteen years ago would be out of business today unless she expanded, because most authors no longer need these services now that they write on desktop computers. Similarly, recession, or inflation, can force a freelancer into expansion or decline.

Anytime, in fact, that you are not earning enough money to support yourself in the style to which you consider yourself to be entitled, the solution is to expand. Often it takes a few years of freelancing to realize that this is what you need to do. But expansion is also a normal, ongoing activity of all businesses. It is what they do to stay viable. If anything, the need to expand is perhaps more pressing for freelancers than for other small businesses because we do not sell products, and we often have a smaller roster of clients than larger businesses.

WHEN IT'S TIME TO GROW

Sometimes an otherwise savvy freelancer tells me his business has dried up for no particular reason that he can see. This happened to Jim Snyder, who had established a cozy and very profitable business installing computers for small-business owners. Jim recalls, "I had set everything up right, made lots of cold calls, and followed up every possible lead. I enjoyed a healthy freelance business for two years. In fact, I never made new calls after the first round that I made to set up my business. People came to me, and it was very nice, since I don't like selling myself, but then, who does? Then one fall, right after a very busy summer, I had no work lined up. I was finishing a project, and for the first time in two years, I wasn't booked months, or even weeks, in advance."

While Jim's business may look like it dried up for no apparent reason, this is not really what happened. It declined because he neglected to take care of one very important function: soliciting new business. Even though Jim doesn't like to sell himself, he needs to do it all the time, as an ongoing process. And sometimes a more serious and formal kind of expansion is called for, one that sends you back to the drawing board in search of an entirely new direction.

Reexamining the Customer Profile

Begin by examining the customer profile you wrote for your business plan. Among other things, it often shows why your business is sinking. To see what has happened to you, as well as what might be a good, new direction, ask and answer the following questions about your customers.

1. Have you developed any special expertise, based on the customers who seek you out? In other words, why do you have the customers you have?
2. Why have you lost customers? Be honest. Was your work unsatisfactory? Did the customers' needs change so much that

your services were no longer required? Did the competition offer some service you could not provide? Did you have to charge too much?

3. What trends can you spot in your present customers' businesses? How will these trends affect the need for your services?
4. Do you want to regain the customers you lost? Never overlook this as a possibility. Freelancers always have some customers who are inactive simply because they have not been called on for a while. On the other hand, do you prefer to find new customers?
5. Which customers pay you the most? Can you expand that type of customer?
6. Which customers pay you the least? Can you afford to drop them so you can make room for higher-paying customers?

PLANNING FOR EXPANSION

After analyzing the customer profile, the next step is to analyze, explore, and develop one or more areas into which you might reasonably and successfully expand. Here are some guidelines to help you do this:

1. Describe your present services.
2. List any closely related services that you might expand into.
3. List less closely related areas that nevertheless might be potential points of expansion.
4. Choose the areas that are most appealing and that hold the greatest promise for profits.
5. Methodically begin to explore each of the possibilities. Use online resources as well as library resources. Talk to experts and potential colleagues about the possibility of expansion. In short, repeat the kind of research you did when you were deciding whether to start your present business.
6. Once you have pinpointed an area of expansion, write a business plan to explore how viable the idea is. Figure out how much the expansion will cost and whether you can afford it.

By following this process, you will make a rational decision about a new direction. And if one plan does not work out, there are usually other avenues to explore.

EXPLORING THE FUTURE

A period of expansion is as good a time as any to reexamine your entire future as a freelancer. In addition to analyzing your new direction, take some time as well to explore the psychological and emotional ramifications of the change you are about to make. Here are some questions to think about:

- Do you want to stay in the industry you are in? Barbara Lee, photographer's representative, has no immediate plans to move, but she knows that she does not want to live in New York City for many more years. And although she enjoys the high earnings of her present business and knows that she will always freelance, she has begun to investigate careers that could be pursued outside New York City. So far she has not found her niche, but she has established some standards. First, she doesn't like record keeping, so the business she enters next must be something she can run on a cash basis with little need for record keeping. She loves animals, so she is looking for some service related to animal care that she could provide. Janet Rish, on the other hand, loves the freelance consulting she does in museums, where she helps to set up shows. The pay is low, though, so she needs to expand in the same business. She is considering how to approach corporations with art collections that could use her services.
- Are you willing to travel to find new markets? Often freelancers tend to forget that there are potential markets everywhere. One enterprising public-relations expert who worked in the beauty business in New York also saw the possibility of freelancing for small salons in nearby cities. The response to her direct mail flyer came from Washington, D.C., and now she thinks of her

monthly jaunts to Washington as one of the perks of her job. Conversely, an excellent freelance editor who specialized in sailing books and lived in Washington, D.C., found her specialized market could be tapped in New York. She made twice-monthly trips to New York to keep in touch with her clients there.

- Do you have enough time? If you are expanding because you cannot earn a good living in your present field, then you may hurt yourself even more if you cut back on the number of hours you work so you can devote yourself to your expansion efforts. The trick is to expand into areas that will not require huge amounts of time, or to grit your teeth and accept the fact that you will live a little poorer than you want to for yet another start-up period.
- Are you emotionally up for this expansion? Expanding a business takes a lot of energy, and it's important to be ready for it. If you are burdened with other problems or are in the midst of another major change, this may not be the opportune moment to expand. Expand when you are feeling good about yourself and your capacity to breathe new life into your business.

THE IMPORTANCE OF NETWORKING

Even when you are not formally expanding your business, it is still important always to be on the lookout for new customers—and to carefully maintain ties to old ones. Following are several fruitful ways to do this:

- Keep up with your field. Read and do on-line research regularly. Not only will this keep your mind alert to new directions, but when you meet new contacts or old ones, you will be able to speak intelligently about trends and ideas.
- Teach. This is an excellent way to put your name out there, as well as a good credential to use with clients.
- Lecture or perform. Like teaching, this puts your name where it needs to be, in front of old and potential clients.

- Join and become active in one or more professional organizations. Every freelancer needs ties like this.
- Occasionally join a group that is slightly off target but close to your area of interest. If you are a freelance editor who does the occasional index, for example, join a professional indexers' group. A nonfiction writer might join a professional association for investigative reporters. One good way to locate these groups is via the Web. Furthermore, many professional groups maintain a Web page and a forum, as well as having an E-mail address. "Joining" groups on the Web is less time-consuming (if also somewhat less social) than going to meetings.
- Think about joining a new generalist group as well, especially one that might produce some new leads for business.
- Do some consulting. Telling others how to do what you do forces you to review what you are doing right and wrong. And it could result in new business.
- Pay attention to present clients. Give a party for them or take one to lunch. These are ties that need to be renewed on a regular, ongoing basis.

DEALING WITH YOUR PRESENT CLIENTS DURING EXPANSION

While you are in the process of moving yourself on to greater glory, do not neglect the people who have been hiring you all along. Rarely will you want to give them up entirely, so your only alternative is to continue to service their accounts while you develop new ones. There is an art to servicing regular clients, though. Do not overservice bread-and-butter accounts, meaning those regular ones who will use you no matter what you do. They are not in the wine-and-dine category because they are already there for you. Do continue, however, to give regular clients very good service.

Do not overservice marginal accounts, either. One freelancer who specialized in writing textbooks by teaming up with someone who had expert knowledge but needed a writer came to the realization that she was courting some of her clients far too much. The jobs she went after were big, often involving sizable advances and a 50 percent cut on royalties, so they did require some courting, which might be drawn out over several months before a deal was struck. Often, though, prospective clients, which included publishers and academics, came to her before they really had a go-ahead on a project. She soon learned to be polite but to give these people a minimal amount of her time until they had something concrete to discuss.

Bailing Out

Finally, if freelancing truly is not working out for you, it simply may be time to bail out, either permanently or temporarily. The freelance life is not for everyone, and there is no disgrace in admitting that you are not cut out for it.

Some people cannot freelance because they lack the personality or the temperament. Unfortunately, sometimes you have to freelance to discover this. One former freelancer, now a happily employed managing editor with a major publisher, thought he had everything he needed to freelance: lots of ambition, an ability to tolerate a considerable amount of time alone, a love of independence. Plus, he hated his job. Offered the chance to freelance full-time, he quit his job the same day, bought some paper and pens, and considered himself in business. He recalls, "Within three months, I knew this wasn't for me. I missed the camaraderie of the office, the excitement of getting up and going to work every day. All the self-discipline I had when I worked for someone else—I always stayed late and took work home—just fell apart when I had to face whole days alone in my apartment. I got a full-time job with the company I was supposed to freelance for as soon as one opened up."

Don't assume you aren't cut out for freelancing, though, simply because you do not like to work alone. If you like what you are doing, and you like working for yourself, then the solution may be to find an office to go to while you work. Many people cannot spend the entire day alone and be productive, but when they are ensconced in an office environment, they do very well. If this sounds like you, before you give up on freelancing, try renting space with other workers so you will have some companionship. Or perhaps you need a partner. There are solutions if this is your problem.

Signs That a Bailout May Be Best

There are some clear indicators, though, that you may not be cut out to freelance. If you answer yes to most of the questions below, it may be time to think about bailing:

- You find yourself barely able to pay the bills month after month.
- Instead of getting up early and eagerly tackling your work, you sleep later and later, take longer and longer lunches, and in short just do not get much done during the day.
- You are bored and feel unchallenged.
- You are lonely, not for a few minutes, but most of the time.
- You are depressed.
- You suffer from anxiety, which many people use to ward off depression.
- You cannot expand your business enough to feel secure should you lose even one major client.
- You cannot earn enough to take vacations. Anyone starting a business may skip vacations for a year or two, but if you have gone for years without a vacation, something is wrong.
- You cannot earn enough to put aside money for retirement.

If most of this list sounds alarmingly like your life, then you are in trouble as a freelancer. Remember, though, that all work is cyclical. Everyone goes through ups and downs, good periods and bad. Be careful not to mistake temporary burnout for burnout that cannot be cured.

Another important way to tell whether you need to find yourself another career is to consider your motives for freelancing. Why do you do it? For the glamour? The free time? The independence? These are not good enough reasons alone to keep you in the business; the work is simply too hard for that.

Furthermore, consider that if you have a need to shine in front of people, a need that has kept you struggling to be an actor for fifteen years with little success, then you will probably apply that need to shine to whatever work you do. Which means you can shine at some other kind of job. Never mistake a love of glamour or a need to have a certain kind of attention for a love of the kind of work you do.

You also may want to reconsider when all your friends are making a lot more money than you are. There is nothing wrong with struggling at a career for a number of years—freelancers and nonfreelancers do that—but when everyone else seems be way out in front of you, that is another sign that it may be time to pull out.

Finally, if you constantly feel stressed or anxious, think about giving it up. The toll anxiety and stress take on your health is not worth it.

Once you contemplate getting out, consider whether this is likely to be a permanent or a temporary move. As one freelancer notes, "I think I'm getting a little bored now, and I might look around for something else to do. But I know that I will freelance at various points throughout my life. Perhaps I have not found the area to freelance in. The idea of freelancing appeals to me, and I've done well at one freelance business. I'm just not sure it is the right business." This feeling is echoed by many freelancers. Just as there are personalities incapable of freelancing, there are also people who have a freelance mentality in the very best sense of the word. Sometimes, these people need a few years to find the right freelance career.

If you think you are leaving freelancing temporarily because of a bad economy or while you look for another area in which to reestablish yourself, then take this into account when you wind down your freelance business.

Making a Successful Exit

Whether you are leaving freelancing temporarily or permanently, there is an art to getting out gracefully.

If you are leaving temporarily, take care not to burn any bridges with your clients. One possibility is to turn your clients over to a colleague, but the disadvantage to doing this is that you may lose your clients permanently to another freelancer. But if this is necessary to ensure good will between you and your clients and to smooth the path for the day when you may return to freelancing, then it may be worth it.

If you decide not to supply your clients with another source of free-lance help, you should still notify them of your plans to leave the free-lancing business. And it may be a smart idea to save all your files and contacts for a return engagement in the freelance business.

It is almost impossible to sell a freelance business, especially a one-person operation. You simply cannot promise someone that he or she will achieve the same volume of business you have, and since the business is based entirely on your ability to sell your services, there is not much else to sell. You can try to sell your contact file, but a smart freelancer knows that the file is accessible for free in other places—such as the public library or on the Web.

If You Decide to Continue Freelancing

If all signs point toward the fact that yours is a successful freelance business, then you probably don't need much advice. A few words will suffice:

- Keep a fairly tight rein on your financial status. Freelancers walk a tightrope between operating in the red and the black. You may always have to watch your financial status carefully.
- Always be on the lookout for new work and new assignments. Remember that there is no better time to look for more work than when you are very busy with your present work. Never count on the same clients using you over and over again. Instead, always keep an eye open for new possibilities.
- Always plan ahead, not only for finding new work and new areas in which to work but also for investing in your future. If you don't handle this, no one else will.
- Always leave a little time for contemplation and self-evaluation. This is the best way to find new directions. Freelancing is the

most flexible career path you can follow. Just be sure that you maintain enough personal flexibility always to be ready for what lies ahead.

The last word: Make sure you are enjoying yourself. Otherwise, the creative endeavors, the long hours, the times when money is tight will not be worthwhile in the long run.

BIBLIOGRAPHY

Albrecht, Karl, and Ron Zemke. *Service America!* New York: Warner Books, 1985. This perennial seller contains lots of trendy yet useful advice on operating a service-driven company.

Albrecht, Karl. *The Only Thing That Matters: Bringing the Power of the Customer into the Center of Your Business.* New York: Harper Business, 1992. While not written specifically for either small businesses or freelancers, this book will show you how to produce satisfied customers. And who knows? The big-business examples contained in its pages may even inspire you.

Bly, Robert W. *Selling Your Services: Proven Strategies for Getting Clients to Hire You (or Your Firm).* New York: Henry Holt, 1992. A thorough guide to selling services, this book has two very helpful chapters, one on closing a sale and another on repeat sales.

Boyan, Lee. *Successful Cold Call Selling.* New York: Amacon, 1989. An excellent all-round book on selling yourself and your services.

Christianson, Stephen G. *Business Law Made Easy.* New York: Doubleday, 1995. This book is useful for its concise and clear explanations of the legal documents that small-business owners will encounter. Especially helpful are the sample documents.

Cohen, Herb. *You Can Negotiate Anything.* New York: Bantam, 1982. This long-selling book tells you everything you need to know to negotiate successfully.

Huff, Priscilla Y. *101 Best Home-Based Businesses for Women: Everything You Need to Know About Getting Started on the Road to Success.* Rocklin, Calif.: Prima Publishing. Basically a catalog of ideas, this book introduces you to the possibilities for home work, which by the way are hardly limited to women.

Kamoroff, Bernard, C.P.A. *Small-Time Operator: How to Start Your Own Business, Pay Your Taxes, and Stay Out of Trouble!* Laytonville, Calif.: Bell Springs Publishing, 1995. Now deservedly in its twentieth edition, this is the granddaddy of good books about self-employment. Dense and not particularly attractive in its layout, it is nevertheless a bible for the self-employed.

Levinson, Jay Conrad. *Guerilla Advertising: Cost-Effective Tactics for Small-Business Success.* New York: Houghton Mifflin, 1994. A good all-round guide with less nitty-gritty practical advice than Smith's book on advertising but still with lots to keep you interested and make you think.

Lonier, Terri. *The Frugal Entrepreneur: Creative Ways to Save Time, Energy, and Money in Your Business.* New Paltz, N.Y.: Portico Press, 1996. Organized in palatable mini-soundbites, this accessible book contains its share of useful information on saving money in everything from hiring to buying office supplies to joining professional organizations.

Parlapiano, Ellen H., and Patricia Cabe. *Mompreneurs: A Mother's Practical Step-by-Step Guide to Work-at-Home.* New York: Perigree, 1996. Don't let the cloying title put you off this very practical guide for home-based entrepreneurs with kids. The many truly practical hints—all directed to mom—will probably work just as well for self-employed, at-home dads.

Sanderson, Steve, ed. *Standard Legal Forms and Agreements for Small Businesses.* Bellingham, Wash.: Self-Counsel Press, Inc., 1990. This book is comprised mostly of documents and descriptions of them, but it is the best guide to the forms you need to operate a freelance business.

Smith, Cynthia. *How to Get Big Results from a Small Advertising Budget.* New York: Lyle Stuart, 1989. This is an excellent book chock-full of solid, useful advice. It tells you where to put your advertising dollar, what not to bother with, and above all, what's realistic for a small operation.

Stewart, Marjabelle Young, and Marian Faux. *Executive Etiquette in the New Workplace.* New York: St. Martin's Press, 1994. Aimed at corporate executives, everything in this book also applies to freelancers.

Tracy, John A. *Budgeting à La Carte: Essential Tools for Harried Business Managers.* New York: John Wiley & Sons, Inc., 1996. At times bordering on too complex, this is still one of the best guides to small-business finance.

Weinstein, Grace W. *Financial Savvy for the Self-Employed.* New York: Henry Holt, 1995. This is a good nuts-and-bolts practical guide to running your own business written by an expert who knows what she is talking about.

INDEX